Overthinking

The Quickest Way to Stop Overthinking Everything You Do - Includes Practical Strategies to Let Go of Fear & Worries

Chase Connor

Table of Contents

Introduction

"If you only do what's urgent, you'll never do what's important." - Margaret Thatcher

We live in a world that is always changing and evolving. As professionals, we are always outgrowing our current skillsets and expanding our expertise to stay competitive and relevant. Taking on new challenges and opportunities can sometimes be overwhelming as it includes some level of risk-taking that is not always calculated or planned. It becomes challenging to stay engaged in learning new things while feeling confident with the old skills we have mastered. We begin to overthink things.

Overthinking is not a bad thing, but it does become bad when you are stuck in the cycle of doing the same thing over and over again while not getting any positive outcomes. It happens to us all. We can get stuck in a rut, and we find ourselves repeating our old patterns of behavior without even realizing it.

It all starts with something seemingly insignificant, like doing the same thing repeatedly, even though it is not working. This could be as trivial as checking your email inbox every night or checking the same news sites on your phone every day. Sometimes, you can get trapped in the mindset of doing things the same way; it feels acceptable because that is how you always have, and that's how you always will.

But there are other times when we can do something mundane every day, but still feel like it was a good choice because it somehow brought us value to our lives, such as going to work, taking care of our homes and family, or spending time with loved ones.

Overthinking can be a good thing in certain aspects of our lives, just as long as we can recognize when it goes from being good to bad. There are times when we are overthinking because we need to think things through or we feel insecure about the decisions we need to make. This type of thinking can be a source of inspiration and creativity too.

What is important is the ability to know what kind of thinking you are doing to discern when it has become destructive versus helpful. You must understand the motivations and intentions behind the thoughts coming into your head. Being able to separate fact from fiction is a crucial part of cultivating healthy thinking that will allow you to stay focused on what is important.

One of the best ways to separate fact from fiction is employing the 7-Second Rule. This rule will help you identify your thoughts and evaluate them based on how realistic they are. It works by challenging you to identify how realistic it is for you to think about something in seven seconds or less. If you can't come up with why your thought isn't realistic in seven seconds, it becomes a distraction that may become a source of stress and anxiety shortly.

It simply boils down to this: by observing the thoughts you are having, you can recognize the difference between fact and fiction. You will be able to assess if it is worth getting upset about or if it just a distraction that can be thrown away.

So, before you start overthinking things in the future, ask yourself these questions:

1. How realistic is my thought? _____

2. Is my thought helping/hurting me? _____

3. How much time am I willing to spend on this thought?
_____

4. How can I get out of this thought soon? _____

5. What is the benefit/cost of doing this thought?
_____

6. How would I look if I did this thought?
_____

7. How will my future be affected by doing this thought? [no, but how am I going to make it better?]
_____ ”

I invite you to read this book to learn how to stop overthinking and start making better decisions in your life.

Chapter 1:
Causes of Overthinking

O verthinking is one of the many ways in which a person can become anxious. It is an unnecessary and daunting task to undertake, as it may not even need to be solved or dealt with. People who overthink will think about things too much and too often and continue to put themselves through mental anguish each time they do. This can lead to a situation where the person cannot function properly, or even at all, due to the immense amount of thought they put into something. Many different things can cause someone to overthink. They may only realize this after the fact or after being told, so it is often overlooked by the individual who is overthinking.

The causes of overthinking vary greatly. It can vary from something simple like a small worry or question to a much more complex issue. Some of the causes of overthinking include:

1. Worrying

Worrying is something that tends to be common among people who overthink. Worrying is a negative thing in itself, as it is unnecessary, and it does not help solve the problem one is worried about. Once the worry has been started, it can be hard to stop or slow down. This is because all the energy that goes towards worrying is wasted energy. It cannot contribute anything in terms of being productive or helping solve any problems. Worrying can happen for small things or larger things; it can even occur over whether there will be enough food to eat at dinner later on that night.

2. Questions

Questions are another cause of overthinking. Frequently, people who overthink tend to ask themselves questions such as "What if I did X?" "How would I react if I did Y?" or "What would that mean for me?" A person may ask over and over again what would happen if they did X and try to predict every possible scenario in their head to figure out the best course of action.

3. Obsession

Obsession can cause a person to think too much about something. People become fixated on one thing, whether it has happened in their past or something they are currently experiencing. Obsessive people often do not notice their obsession, and they will continue to think about whatever they are obsessed with. Obsessive thoughts tend to go into overthinking, where the person is completely lost in their head and often starts talking to themselves.

4. Loss of Focus

Loss of focus can cause a person to start thinking too much about things or events that might not necessarily be important. The idea of losing focus can frighten many people who do not want their minds to wander off and begin thinking about anything and everything that comes into their heads. It is not necessarily bad for thoughts to wander and the mind to go elsewhere, but when the mind wanders, one becomes lost in thought and doesn't stop.

5. Over Identification

Over identification can cause a person to become too attached or overly invested in a certain subject or person. This can be something as simple as one being confused by feelings towards someone or something as complicated as feeling that one is responsible for every decision they make (especially if it's an important one). People who overidentify tend to think a lot about their feelings towards something without realizing the amount of time they put into it. This can cause them to become lost in thought, and they might not even notice the time they have spent over thinking something so small.

6. Organizing

Organizing thoughts is another cause of overthinking. People who organize their thoughts will often put a lot of time into planning out their days and the things they need to do, or even just planning what they are going to do. Overthinking occurs when these people have too much on their minds. They will try to plan everything that happens in their lives and try to predict every outcome of what may happen if X happened rather than Y.

7. Thinking Too Much

Thinking too much is a bit of a broad topic, but there are many different reasons. A person might not know what to think about or what is going on in their lives. This can be anything from someone who does not know when to stop thinking to someone who has too much on their mind and doesn't know where to begin to get those thoughts out of their head. Thinking too much often leads a person to overthink because they are trying so hard and obsessing over every single little thing going on in their lives.

8. Control

People who are overly concerned with controlling everything around them will often overthink out of fear that they might not control as much as they would like. These people will sometimes overthink because they are afraid of what would happen if something changed or how much control they would have if something went in a different direction. Frequently, it isn't even about the control itself; the person is more worried about what being without control might mean for them and how it would impact their lives.

9. Confusion

Confusion can easily cause a person to begin overthinking as well. The confusion of not understanding things clearly can cause a person to feel unsure of what is going on and begin overthinking things that they did not know about. This could be something as simple as not knowing if a major event would happen in their lives or if they would be happy doing something particular. It often leads to overthinking that something out of the ordinary will happen, then leading to endless wandering thoughts in their head. These people are often thought of as high-strung because they worry about everything.

10. Trying Too Hard

Trying too hard to do something you are unsure of will often cause a person to overthink. For example, it could be a person trying to impress someone. They may overthink what led them to do one thing or another, rather than just thinking about what they wanted out of the situation. They might also overthink things out of fear that they are not trying hard enough, or that someone else is doing better, or they might fail if it turns out that they were not doing as good a job. The same goes for people in sports or other activities. They are doing an activity well, so if they do poorly, they end up overthinking things rather than just letting things happen and realizing that it was okay and part of normal life.

11. Perfectionism

People who are perfectionists tend to overthink because they want everything to be 100% right before going ahead and doing anything. This means that everything has to end up being perfect in their minds, or it might not be okay. These people will often overthink every little bit of something before it even happens so there is no room for error. It can be so bad that they will think about things far in advance to ensure they are perfect before they go ahead. They can even drive themselves into excessive worrying because they have to feel a certain way too often for their own good. If someone is not careful, overthinking like this can turn into an obsession.

12. Anticipating Problems

Many people overthink because they are afraid of what might happen if certain things happen. For example, if someone thinks their partner will walk out or cheat on them, they may end up overthinking things constantly when it comes to this person. They may even try and second guess what might happen in advance so as to be prepared for it. This kind of thinking can cause one to become a paranoid.

13. Fear of Failing

This is very common, where someone wonders if they will fail at something before they even begin. This person is afraid they won't be able to do something as well as they should because they are worried about failing. So, this person usually tries not to think about things because of how much it stresses them out.

14. A little too old for their age

If you've ever heard the term "old soul," this is usually what it refers to. This person is usually quite mature, or at least wise way beyond their years because they have been examining and contemplating the world around them from a very young age. They will understand many concepts and ideas that younger people do not understand yet, simply because they have been learning about them for so long.

15. Thinking too much about dead people

Thinking too much about someone who has died, or that they will die can result in reading too much into things to make sure that everything is going to be alright.

16. Overthinking things that happened in the past

This can cause a person to stop living in the present and become very concerned with what has already happened or may have happened. The mind goes back and forth between the past and the present because one cannot change what has already happened.

Overthinking is a part of life for many people. In the areas of philosophy, psychology, and sociology, it has been studied extensively. Some studies have shown no significant differences between how men and women process their thoughts. However, some studies have shown that men are more likely to recognize mental disorders in themselves, while women are less likely to do so.

In modern times, overthinking is often viewed as a poor coping mechanism or a sign of being overwhelmed with stress or pressure; however, this is not always the case. Many people decide to overthink certain things for many different reasons. Most of the time, those who overthink tend not to be mentally ill but are simply using coping methods to deal with stress or pressure.

Overthinking is a function of the mind that often occurs at inappropriate times and is not used in beneficial ways. Those who overthink usually become lost in thought because they are unable to stop thinking, and when they do attempt it, they find that their thoughts are going in circles. They never actually come up with any solutions. Overthinking tends to cause severe mental stress and can potentially lead to severe psychological disorders such as depression, anxiety disorders, mood disorders, and even psychosis.

Since this can be dangerous, people who overthink often try to avoid it by shunning certain situations or people. Unfortunately, this is usually not the best way to go about things because it is extremely difficult to avoid every situation or person completely. Still, at least they can be prepared if they encounter something they know will cause them to think too much.

For example, suppose someone believes that they will likely experience a panic attack in a meeting and try their best not to think about it. In that case, chances are that they will never actually end up having one and therefore won't have been forced into thinking too much. But if we want to avoid overthinking, we need to stop doing whatever is causing us to do it in the first place. The best way is by being self-reflective, which means we need to recognize where our minds tend to wander and, most importantly, when we are overthinking.

There are many different ways that people cope with stress and pressure like expressing emotions and feelings through speaking out loud (which helps many solve their issues) or writing out a list of things that can be done or undone so they don't have a problem in the first place. If you find it hard to stop thinking about something, try a meditation technique such as a breathing exercise or even focus on your current activity. You can also try some distracting activity such as playing a video game or reading a book. Doing these things requires thinking about them, which means that we will be less likely to think about those things that cause us pain or stress.

Alternatively, you can choose not to worry and accept the problem. For example, if you are worried about something but know there is nothing you can do about it, just don't worry about it. Suppose the situation doesn't change or get any better; then worrying will be pointless in the long run. Some people choose to make themselves feel better by taking action or learning more information on the subject but if this causes you pain, taking action is not always the best way to go about things.

It's important to remember that overthinking is a normal and healthy part of life because it allows us to learn and grow towards maturity. If you find yourself overthinking about something, try and analyze why this is happening and what you can do to stop it because overthinking can be one of the most destructive things we can do to ourselves.

It's important to understand that when we start thinking too much, we are not suffering from an illness; instead, our minds are trying to prevent us from doing something that will cause us pain later on or keep us from achieving something big.

Chapter 2:
Symptoms of Overthinking

When I am in San Francisco, I like to go to a café in Japan Town. It's a quiet, dark little café with an excellent mocha latte and unreliable internet that prevents me from getting too distracted from the book I'm reading – or writing. But is good enough to search for the basics in Google. I usually spend a couple of hours there, and then I go to a nearby grocery store to buy some sushi makis for lunch. After a few occasions, I discovered that I always get the same things: one plate of tuna makis and one of salmon makis.

The thing is, I don't really like tuna that much. I like salmon much more. Still, for the sake of variety, I buy both instead of buying only salmon makis. If I had to choose only one plate, I'd choose the salmon. If I choose only one plate, I'd choose salmon both times. Why do I end up buying tuna, then?

For the sake of variety? What variety? Why is variety even better? Do I buy them because this is how I show appreciation for salmon makis? If I only had salmon makis, all would be the same, sitting on a relatively low place on my personal scale of worth. However, having only half salmon makis makes them more valuable. You may wonder, "Okay, salmon makis, got it, but where are you heading with this crazy brainstorm?"

Let me get to the point. Having this seemingly useless mental chatter on my way back to the café after lunch made me realize something.

Mental chatter and clutter are necessary to make you satisfied. If you only think about valuable information, none of your thoughts would be truly valuable. Some mental chatter gives true value to the good thoughts. You appreciate good thoughts more because they are scarcer and pop out amid your nonsensical mental chatter.

Does the nonsense make you feel weird sometimes? Sure, it does. But this weirdness is also part of you. Searching for a slightly less wrong answer through your emotional memory arsenal is not a bad thing. Without thinking about something, you won't find answers. That way you'll accept others' "truth" that will inevitably feel foreign, make you feel uncomfortable and turn on your brain-munching bug of overthinking.

Let me clarify it. This kind of inner chatter is the purest, most innocent instinctive voice of yours. This voice has a childish curiosity, a willingness to discover and understand the world for your benefit, not to mess your life up. If you want a visual picture about it, this voice is the proverbial angel on your right shoulder. It's the voice of your true personality, part of those little quirks and perks that make you - you. This relentless pure chatter will give birth to some great ideas that take you forward instead of holding you back.

You know how can you distinguish "helpful mental chatter" from that compulsory feeling of overthinking? Helpful mental chatter is followed by action. Overthinking serves mostly to avoid taking action.

There's a weird paradox in our overthinking system. We overthink because if something is not complicated, it doesn't seem challenging enough, and we attach little value to it. It's not worthy of action. As soon as we overcomplicate it, we fail taking action because it then scares us.

Some people know what they are supposed to do, but they simply don't act. Others get stuck in analysis paralysis to avoid failure and pain. However, avoiding pain and failure is not helpful. It eliminates the chance to learn. Not knowing the future, a failure today can become a great success tomorrow, if you let it.

Ditch the analysis paralysis, and make decisions instead. Whatever decision you make will bring you somewhere. It can be a place for success or a place to learn. Yet, failing to make a decision means you failed to learn and grow. Now and then you'll hit proverbial forks in the road. When this happens, you may think you have two options, going left or going right. The Minimalists, Joshua Fields Millburn and Ryan Nicodemus, argue that you have not two but four choices when it comes to an existential crossroads.

The first option is what they call "the right path". This is the path of an obvious right decision. There are no questions related to this road. It is like Broadway, surrounded by trees, illuminated, and fireworks sparking all around. There are choices like, "Should I kill my broker for mismanaging my money or shall I solve this issue peacefully within the borders of the law?" Obviously, the first option is a no-no.

The other side of the obvious choices is called "the wrong path". Choices here are blatantly wrong. If you have a little reason, conscience or sensibility, you avoid these routes. Sometimes they may seem quite tempting, like telling your annoying boss that "she's an ugly witch with serious sociopath manners, it's no wonder she doesn't have a husband." Taking revenge on her in such a manner is a very attractive option, but you and I both know that you're much better than that.

The Minimalists call the third type of choice one can make "the left path". In many cases, one path seems right but so does the other. Maybe you cannot tell which path is the better one. Maybe one would be good short term, the other long term. Like the translation offer I once received: X dollars advance plus ten percent royalty, or no advance but twenty percent royalty. Clearly, for the short term, the first option sounded more tempting. Who cares about a five-year reward when I can spend the earnings today? In these cases, the best choice is to collect all the pros and cons for both options. Why today? Because who knows what tomorrow brings. You can't know what your future self will wish. If you picked right, good job. If you picked wrong, learn from it. I picked the second option, by the way, the long-term twenty percent. Why? Based on my needs of today, I didn't need quick money, fortunately. Since I didn't know how I would stand financially in five years, that twenty percent secure savings gives me peace of mind. In my case, long term investment was a pro of today.

The fourth choice is to make no choice at all. When we look at two unknown possibilities, we often freeze and start overthinking them, get into analysis paralysis to avoid taking action and failure. Not making a decision is also a decision, but it is the worst kind. It will keep you stuck.

Why shouldn't you worry about your decisions too much. I could answer this with a simple cliché, like you are just some small dust in the endless eternity of the universe. Your decisions don't usually make any significant change to the big picture, so don't take yourself so seriously. Well, if I were looking for an answer, and read a book that served me with something I just said, I'd be very grateful because I knew with what to light my first fire come winter.

Here is another, less clichéd answer that might actually help your decision-making mind monster. Decisions that we have to make each day are connected to one single frame of time, our future. As a matter of fact, there is no other species on earth that anticipates future events like humans do. Squirrels may save nuts for winter, migratory birds might fly south, but their squirrel and bird brains don't construct their futures like ours do. They are simple; driven by basic instinct, and sensing a decrease in temperature, they know that it is time to do what they have coded in their nature. They put together present events (I feel cold) with past events (last time I stayed here for too long when it was cold, I almost froze) to "predict" a possible consequence for the future.

Their brain doesn't jump to conclusions based on conscious thoughts, only purely instinctual ones. Daniel Gilbert in his bestselling book, Stumbling on Happiness, calls this kind of predictions "nexting". What is nexting? It's an alternative made-up word that refers to predictions such as the squirrel's nut scavenging habits. Decisions like that are short-term triggered by the here and now. They are not far-reaching predictions like stock market changes, the next dominant musical or painting style, or Taylor Swift's next boyfriend. Nexting is a chain of decision-making in the present moment.

Every moment you are make a nexting type of decision. Now, for example you're reading my lines nexting about where this thought about nexting is going. It is nexting when you take your umbrella instinctively when you see clouds outside. Nexting is completing a sentence that starts with "my heart will go on". If we humans could only do nexting, we wouldn't be any different than a canary in a cage. The canary doesn't have any sense about the future; it just peacefully twitters, swinging on its little swing. When it's hungry, it squeaks loudly because it knows that food will follow. The reflex of the bird's brain is built on the angry owner's lack of patience.

We are different. An unprecedented growth doubled the size of the brain of our ancestors, making the one-and-a-quarter-pound brain of the homo habilis into the nearly three-pound brain of the homo sapiens. Breaking down this growth into different areas, a disproportionate growth affected what we call the frontal lobe. This part of the brain, as you might have guessed from its name, is positioned above the eyes, in the front of the skull. (C. A. Banyas, "Evolution and Phylogenetic History of the Frontal Lobes", pg. 83-106)

In the 1800s, psychologists and neurologists assumed that the frontal lobe was a good-for-nothing part of the brain which if it gets injured changes nothing in a person's behavior. Later, in the early 1900s, this opinion slightly changed. Following experiments made on monkeys, they observed that in lobotomizing them (chemically or mechanically destroying some parts of the frontal lobe), the animals became much calmer afterwards. The animals previously outraged if their food was withheld now patiently waited for their portion. A Portuguese physician, António Egas Moniz, tried the method on human patients in the mid 1900s to treat anxiety and depression. They experienced the same effect as the monkeys. They felt much calmer. (D. Gilbert, "Stumbling on Happiness", pg. 13-14.)

As a matter of fact, they were very calm, not having any worry in the world. The breakthrough discovery of the next decades regarding the damage to the frontal lobe stated that people lost their ability to think about the future. Patients with frontal lobe damage seemed unchanged as long as they didn't have to make any predictions about the future so they didn't have to plan. What's common in planning and anxiety? They are both future-related. Scientists today admit that humans without a healthy frontal lobe are like canaries, trapped in the eternal present, unable to "consider the self's extended existence throughout time." (Gilbert, pg. 15.)

The frontal lobe, the youngest part of our brain, makes long-term planning happen. Long-term plans are those that require our attention to choose one of the four types of decisions we can make (preferably number one and three, choosing the right or left thing). Making these long-term decisions shouldn't worry us too much – and not because we're just dust in the wind.

It is because we don't know our future selves. Your future self is like an ungrateful child. It doesn't matter how much you struggle in making the best possible decisions for the future you, as it won't be enough. Whatever you consider the best for your future self today, in a few years it will seem rather odd or dull. And that's good. It means you grew. You have a wider perspective and you are less wrong about things than you were a few years before.

This doesn't mean you shouldn't choose the best option possible that your today's mind can conceive of for your future self, but don't overthink it. Take it easy because chances are your future self "will know it better" anyway. Do you ever recall opinions you had a while ago that today seem totally nutty? Yes, that's your current self-trashing your past self, who, guess what, made the best decision you could make at that moment.

I was a late bloomer. I truly believed that my first relationship would be the last and we'd always be together, having a vegetable garden and dogs. When we broke up, I thought I'd never love again. With my second girlfriend, I thought this love was not how love was supposed to look like, like there was a standard for love. I was full of weird thoughts and decisions that as I thought then served my best interests. Today I can only laugh about them. When my first girlfriend broke up with me, I was devastated. I decided to believe that I'd never be okay again – and was I ever wrong.

I remember how frozen, broken and depressed I was when I decided to break up with my second girlfriend. I thought the sorrow would never cease, and I would never be happy. Wrong again. Those decisions that were so painful and difficult for my past self were the best things that ever happened to my present self. The rule works the other way around too. Present tragedies can turn into future successes.

Put that frontal lobe to work on the best future you can conceive of today, but don't overestimate its decision's effect on your long-term life. Don't overload your mind with worries. Don't try to foresee what your future self will want. Don't overthink your options. Use the best of whatever you have now, and make a choice based on those values. Your future self may or may not like your choices of today, but your heart in present will be at peace. That's the only thing you can aim to control.

Chapter 3:

Deal with Procrastination

T he definition of procrastination is widely accepted as delaying or avoiding action or decision. While this definition is accurate, as with the definition of overthinking, it is also overly simplistic when trying to understand procrastination as a psychological concern. It is a major factor and common practice for those who also struggle with controlling their tendency to overthink.

What Is Procrastination and Where Does it Come From?

More than just a popular word in the English vocabulary, procrastination is a negative habit that has existed and been recorded since the early days of humanity. Most prevalently connected with a Greek poet, Hesiod, one famous view of the human impulse to procrastinate was published as "work prospers with care; he who postpones wrestles with ruin." The word "procrastinate" originally comes from the Latin term procrastinate, which translates to "put off until tomorrow." The psychological theory connected to the word "procrastination" comes more from the early Greek phrase, akrasia, which means doing something against one's better instinct or judgment.

This is a repetitive theme amongst procrastinators regardless of location, situation, age, or experience: even while they put off their responsibilities, they know there will be consequences to face if they are not able to get it done in time or when it is expected to be resolved.

However, this knowledge is not enough to inspire action or decision, instead it only serves to fuel the procrastination habit by putting the individual in a deeper and more tumultuous emotional state that only continues to strengthen the urge to hide from the current situation. As their deadline or time limit grows ever closer, they begin to remember their real-life responsibilities and consequences, and panic sets in. Now they fully realize the amount of work they need to get it done and their decision begins to weigh heavy on their shoulders. They rush to get everything completed and come to a solution for what they been procrastinating.

In many cases, they cannot complete it and have to face the real consequences such as having to work off the clock or request an extension. Their dedication to their position is called into question by their superiors. In some cases, however, procrastinators do get everything completed. Instead of regretting their decision to procrastinate, they convince themselves that they do their best work under such pressures, and the habit is born.

Famous Sayings Related to Procrastination

"Don't put off until tomorrow what you can do today." - Benjamin Franklin

While we waste our time hesitating and postponing, life is slipping away." - Roman philosopher, Seneca

The first quote is intended to help individuals reach their full potential by inspiring them to take more control over their actions and get themselves moving today. This may work for some as a personal mantra or a reminder not on their office wall, but for those who struggle with procrastination as a compulsion and habit, quotes like Mr. Franklin's have very little effect. Seneca's quote, on the other hand (and the poem it comes from) serves to remind individuals that procrastinating does nothing but waste the time and energy that could be spent on other activities.

One of the most common misconceptions connected with procrastination is that it is a matter of laziness or a lack of discipline. Th is that procrastination has nothing to do with how much self-control a person has. This chapter will cover the finer details of procrastination and reveal some surprising facts about the condition and how it affects men and women of all ages.

Pro Tip: Art is a great way to analyze and process difficult emotions or thoughts! It exercises the creative part of the brain, which helps with its emotional control and strengthening over time. Using art as a means of emotion and thought processing in obsessive or compulsive overthinking gives individuals a unique, productive, and effective way of expressing their thoughts, desires, goals, fears, and other factors or variables for help with understanding and controlling.

Why is Procrastination a Hot Issue When it Comes to Understanding and Conquering Overthinking?

Procrastination is something that all adults wrestle with throughout their lives. However, just because it is a widespread habit does not mean that it is natural or healthy for those who procrastinate regularly or compulsively. The negative side effects take a severe toll on a person's mental and emotional health. One of the main reasons is that most people looking for answers on how to beat their procrastination have enough psychological self-awareness to know how unproductive and hindering the habit can be. They can see how behaviors like procrastination and overthinking are holding them back from reaching their full potential. Even with this knowledge, they cannot make themselves take action or make any solid decisions. Throughout each of their procrastination processes, this knowledge eats away at their self-esteem, causing them to feel even worse and more stressed out as their deadline approaches and the pressure increases.

It isn't just the mind that feels the effects of procrastination over time. The long-term negative effects of this habit can be damaging psychologically and emotionally. It can affect people physically as stress levels (and the physical body processes connected to stress like blood pressure levels and breathing speed) fluctuate into unsafe regions. This fluctuation and inconsistency can lead to muscle weakness (especially in the heart) and even blood clots in more extreme cases.

Many psychological professionals are interested in procrastination and overthinking as serious health concerns, with some even going as far as to categorize them as self-harm behaviors. These behaviors and related habits are getting more attention as depression, anxiety, and suicidal numbers increase across the globe. The more information gathered and studies performed on habits like overthinking and procrastination, the more society as a whole will be able to understand the difficulties related to these conditions and the more solutions can be found for those who have had trouble finding the answers they need for their specific concerns.

The Difference Between Habitual Procrastination and Poor Time Management Skills

One criticism that procrastinators often hear is that they would not be as stressed or pressured in life if they knew how to use their time better. While this seems like a logical solution to a notorious problem for burning energy and letting time pass inefficiently, when it comes down to it, poor time management and procrastination are not the same issues.

Those with poor time management skills have a much easier path ahead of them when stopping the delay or avoidance of their responsibilities and replacing them with better and more productive habits. In many cases, poor time management impulses come from a lack of knowledge about how best to prioritize or organize time to reach the most efficient and productive level. Once these individuals learn the necessary skills to take control of their time management behaviors, they may find themselves procrastinating from time to time. Still, now it is not related to their inability to see the problem as a whole or develop a plan to accomplish their goals in an effective and reasonable timeframe.

Procrastination is different in that many people who are aware that they struggle with procrastinating in various aspects of their life are also aware that they possess the time management skills that should be helping them through every episode of procrastination.

Pro Tip: Take the time to analyze your behaviors or the behaviors of someone you are concerned is struggling with procrastination. If there are tasks that can be planned out or put together with little to no additional stress, this is a good sign that this person already has effective time management skills. However, if they avoid taking action or making any starting motion on their plan, this person is most likely having difficulty overcoming habitual procrastination. If the person being analyzed is you, you have already made a major accomplishment in conquering your procrastination habit: accepting the issue as reality and recognizing the damaging behaviors that make it such a concerning habit.

If you are concerned about someone else's habitual procrastination or lack of time management skills, the best course of action once you have identified their particular behaviors and habits is to speak openly with the person about your concerns. This conversation may help them see the problem in a new light, knowing that others have been able to see it, which may also help them understand and accept the challenge they face. Like any trial or challenge, there is no way to help someone change their ways (even if it would be the best course of action) until they are willing to admit, accept and begin to learn about their condition and where it comes from.

Those unwilling to accept their chronic procrastination often do so because they are not currently under stress, are feeling fine, or are in a positive frame of mind. In this mental state, procrastinators will justify their actions or push them to the back of their minds until their mood starts to slip to the more negative end of the spectrum and the overthinking spiral starts.

The Health Dangers and Other Negative Effects of Procrastination

There are as many different types of effects and dangers associated with procrastination as there are types of personalities. While some may be common or at least reported in various situations and studies, each person has their struggle and individual variables that cause and fuel their procrastination, so not every person will experience each of the different negative effects in a way that makes a lasting impact (or at all).

Loss of Time: One of the most obvious negative effects of procrastination is the amount of time allowed to pass or be burned on unproductive tasks. Some people say this is not directly connected with procrastination but with a person's time management skills (a disconnect many psychologists support as studies show that procrastination and poor time management skills are not necessarily the same issue or even connected in some cases). There are those procrastinators who are lucky enough to have enough trivial tasks or things they're meant to do to occupy their procrastination time, but those who do not spend this time searching for something to do to appear productive so that they justify their procrastination to their logical selves in some way.

Loss of Energy: Many may see procrastination as a form of laziness, but the truth is that the amount of energy it takes to procrastinate is often more exhausting on the mind and body than just doing the task or making a decision. Instead of getting done what they need to finish, procrastinators spend massive amounts of energy on anxious behaviors such as pacing or wasting energy up at night overthinking about their responsibilities and how they need to get them done, keeping the person from getting enough sleep to restore the energy they're wasting on the stress and the panic that comes with procrastination.

Track Record of Bad Decisions: Procrastinators often struggle with regret and obsess over past decisions during their overthinking episodes that only make them feel worse about themselves and their abilities over time. When people doubt themselves, they become less concerned with thinking about their options or trying to plan things out because they lose hope and begin to believe that anything they chose to do will end poorly, so why to bother putting time and energy into weighing the options.

When decisions are made in this mindset, people are not concerned with potential consequences, figuring any path is full of them, so pick one and roll with the punches. Their low self-esteem leads to a lack of hope, motivation, and passion over the years. This behavior can become habitual over time. People who are not concerned with the benefits or consequences of their actions have very little chance of building a successful future.

Damage to Reputation: This could be professionally or personally as one behavior often associated with procrastination is making promises or plans only to break or cancel them at the last minute. Professionally, this could ruin someone's career if allowed to get out of hand. Personally, many people who wrestle with procrastination impulses have ended up alienating themselves from friends and loved ones by avoiding or skipping social situations.

Long-term Negative Health Risks: The stress and sleeping issues that affect procrastinators are ways that procrastination damages people's health. Individuals who struggle with procrastination in their personal and professional lives are more inclined to let the habit seep into other aspects of their lives, such as exercising and going to the doctor. Skipping as a habit starts innocently enough, typically with the individual missing a regular exercise session or a planned lesson for a reasonable circumstance. Sometimes this circumstance or change may be out of the person's control. The issue is not that they have missed the one workout. The issue is that everything was okay while they missed that one exercise window. They may have felt better that day than normally after exercising because they are not all sore and sweaty. This positive feeling is remembered the next time they don't feel like exercising, and the procrastination habit takes control.

Adults should attend regular annual check-ups with their doctors when health concerns start to worry them. Procrastinators often avoid going to the doctor under nearly any circumstance, and others make appointments with the best intentions only to skip them when the time comes. One of the most repeated excuses for procrastinators with this habit is that they feel fine at the moment and the appointment is time that could be used on the task or responsibility they have been procrastinating on. Using their favored reasoning or justification, they talk themselves out of getting their check-up, canceling their appointments often, never reschedule them until an emergency or their loved ones hold an intervention.

Other negative health effects that have been linked to chronic procrastination include:

-heart damage, particularly for individuals already at risk of heart disease for lifestyle or genetic reasons.

-inconsistent sleep patterns that lead to mental and emotional stress and burnout throughout the day.

-damage to emotional health and wellbeing with continuous trials and suffering of the emotions and psychological processes on an individual as they try to beat or justify their procrastination tendencies.

Once procrastinators see the health risks and potential dangers associated with chronic procrastination, many are more likely to be willing to start taking steps toward taking control of the impulses and psychological compulsions commonly practiced with their condition. Now that we've covered the health risks, keep reading for a closer look at some of the most common warnings signs and indicative behaviors seen in procrastinators of all ages.

What are Actions, Signs and Indicators of Procrastination in Men & Women?

The good news for procrastinators everywhere is that anyone can stop procrastinating with some patience and practice and start living to their full potential! One way to accomplish this is first by checking for warning signs or indicators in oneself or others to determine whether they are a chronic procrastinator or someone who struggles with time management.

They Are Often Distracted: Those who fall into the category of habitual procrastinators often struggle in social situations as they tend to be distracted, looking for topics, conversations, or activities they can take part in to avoid whatever task or responsibility they are procrastinating. One of the most prevalent indicators of a procrastinator is the habit of searching for distractions. These are the more active procrastinators who cannot talk themselves into getting a specific task done but are also having trouble letting time pass without productivity. These procrastinators will often make lists of other tasks they meant to get done or less important tasks that they convince themselves they can knock out quickly by focusing all of their attention on one main issue. Their past experiences with procrastination and the negative side effects they've had to deal with tell these procrastinators that they are setting themselves up for unnecessary stress or even failure, but the compulsion to avoid tasks or make decisions is more powerful than logical thoughts.

They Are Often Overwhelmed by a New Task or Assignment: Procrastination is a habit directly tied to emotional and psychological impulses, factors, and desires, depending upon the individual. This is why many chronic procrastinators overreact or give into rising feelings of panic or frustration whenever they are presented with a new responsibility, tasks, or opportunity. Even if it is something that will positively affect them, either through the process of completing it or once the activity or solution in question is reached, many procrastinators only see the negative side of it:

-More work

-Something else to do

-Another decision to make or another plan they have to come up with

Whatever an individual's specific reasons or excuses, their first reaction to new situations is often an emotional one triggered by stress and fear that affects their thoughts and behaviors in ways that make them difficult to work with or even be around.

They Have Difficulty Dealing with Unexpected Changes or Disruptions: One thing procrastinator are often good at is making plans for what they need to get done within a specific timeframe. In most cases, it is the only way to justify their procrastination because they know they have a solid plan of action laid out for when they are ready to get started. This action plan is often their only comfort and fallback when the panic from time constraint or pressure starts to take its toll, and they begin to regret their procrastinating.

This is why when unexpected difficulties, tasks, or decisions arise, procrastinators often have difficulty emotionally or logically handling the change because they most likely did not plan any spare or free space in their timeframe for anything to go sideways or come up. Planning additional time is not something that procrastinators think about, although many adults already possess time management skills. It is an invaluable part of the organization and preparation for any task that people make sure to leave room for the uncertainty that something could disrupt even their best-laid plans.

They Have a Bad Habit of Showing Up Late: Whether it is to work, class or social events, habitual procrastinators are often known in their professional or social groups as the person who likely to show up not only late and most likely unprepared for whatever they are facing that day. This bad habit leads to a reputation of unreliability that can damage relationships.

The habit of being late regardless of the consequence or importance gives procrastinators a disadvantage when building their futures. It gives them a reputation for being unreliable that can penetrate all aspects of their lives from their professional responsibilities to their social, familial, or romantic relationships. Since they are always late, or at least late often enough that others have begun to notice or remark on it as their normal behavior, they are not as trusted as their peers or other members of their group. They often alienate others over time or start to get left out of events and gatherings since people have started to assume the individual would bail anyway. It is not just personal relationships that are be affected. Work superiors may observe this habit of being late and see it as a weakness in the employee. The person then finds themselves missing opportunities or getting passed up for projects or assignments that could further their career.

They Focus on Trivial or Non-Essential Activities Before Getting Necessary Tasks Completed: One of the most common traits displayed by habitual procrastinators is a strong reliance (even a dependence) on lists for organization, regardless of whether they are habitual procrastinators at home or work. The lists themselves can range in length or priority but are typically filled with smaller tasks or lighter decisions that the individual may have been thinking about for some time but are using as a means of distraction from the more pressing tasks they are procrastinating with.

The only thing about these lists is that while they may be informative and impressive at first glance, if someone were to investigate how many of those tasks have actually been marked off or even started, they would be sorely disappointed. Despite their lists, preparation, and organization, most procrastinators never end up checking off their entire lists, or even the majority of the items. Of course, this varies from person to person and how out of control the procrastination impulses are. Still, it is one of the few behaviors that most habitual procrastinators share as it gives them viewable proof to use against people who question their productivity.

Procrastination Habits Identified: What Can Be Done to Help Fix and Solve or Come to Terms with the Issue as a Whole?

The first step in finding a solution to any problem is to understand how it started and how it connects to overthinking. While many people find that the cause of their procrastination is similar to others working to conquer the same matter, every individual will have their variables and specific situations that set them on a different path to understanding and overcoming their struggle.

Chapter 4:

How to Deal with Anxiety

S ocial phobia concerns an extreme fear that eventually creates consistent and long-term feelings of inferiority, inadequacy, embarrassment, self-consciousness, depression, and humiliation. Individuals who become anxious in an irrational manner in social contexts but appear composed and rational alone are probably manifesting social anxiety. Social anxiety was formerly known as social phobia. Globally, an estimated 7% of the population suffers from social anxiety and the lifetime prevalence rate for manifesting social anxiety is 13% to 14%.

Equally important is that social anxiety can be specific or generalized. An example of specific social anxiety may include the fear of speaking in front of groups. An example of generalized social anxiety includes feeling nervous, anxious, and uncomfortable in almost all contexts. Most individuals with social anxiety have a generalized type of social anxiety. Generalized social anxiety manifests as depression, anticipatory anxiety, indecision, worry, and self-blame across most life situations.

In most cases, social anxiety starts during the teenage years and may improve when they get older, but for most people, it persists irrespective of age. In particular, social anxiety is more than shyness as it is an intense fear that does not ease and affects routine activities, relationships, self-confidence, and work. Most people occasionally worry about social situations, but people with social anxiety feel highly worried before and after them.

An individual with social anxiety will fear routine activities such as starting conversations, meeting strangers, working, speaking on the phone, or shopping. One will worry or avoid social activities that include group conversations, parties, and eating with a company if they have social anxiety. People who always worry about doing something they feel are embarrassing, such as sweating, blushing, or appearing incompetent, may exhibit social anxiety. If you have social anxiety, you will find it challenging to accomplish things when others are watching, as you may feel you are being watched and judged all the time.

Additionally, social anxiety makes one fear criticism, shun eye contact, or show low self-esteem. Social anxiety tends to make one feel sweaty, sick, tremble, or experience a pounding heartbeat known as palpitations. Having panic attacks, one experiences an overwhelming sense of anxiety and fear lasting for a few minutes. Most individuals with social anxiety also have other mental health issues such as body dysmorphic disorder, depression, and generalized anxiety disorder.

In brief, one should seek help if they feel they have social anxiety and it is having a significant impact on their lives. Social anxiety is a common problem, but fortunately, there are effective interventions to reverse its effects. Like any mental health condition, most people feel reluctant to ask for help, but most health practitioners are aware that most people are affected and will gladly help. General practitioners may start by asking about their behaviors, feelings, and symptoms to determine more about the anxiety in the patient's social situations.

Notably, social anxiety is beyond shyness, as it is a strong fear of avoiding people and other social interactions. Unlike social anxiety, shyness is a mild fear and does not significantly affect the quality of life that one lives. Most people get a mild fear before meeting new people, but most people easily cope and even enjoy the interaction once the interaction starts. However, when we become captive to intense fear, it becomes a phobia, and it is for this reason that social anxiety was initially called social phobia. The intense and unjustified fear exhibited in social anxiety is mainly due to worrying that people may be critical of you and that you might do something embarrassing.

With general anxiety, one worries that other people are looking at them and taking note of what one is doing. A person with social anxiety will dislike being introduced to other people and find it challenging to go into restaurants or shops. If one worries about eating or drinking in public, then the person is exhibiting social anxiety. People who feel embarrassed about attending public events such as festivals, ceremonies, meetings, and sports may exhibit social anxiety. Expectedly, an individual with social anxiety has difficulties being assertive.

Correspondingly, people with social anxiety may hover around the venue without entering, as they feel not ready to join in. Some individuals with social anxiety may think they are claustrophobic when they are not. When a person exhibiting social anxiety manages to enter a hall where they are people, they tend to feel as though everyone is staring at them. Some individuals with social anxiety wrongly use alcohol to overcome the anxiety, which is counterproductive.

Specific social anxiety affects individuals who want to be the center of attraction, such as teachers, actors, musicians, and teachers. Unlike generalized social anxiety, people with specific social anxiety can relate with other people satisfactorily. However, a person with specific social anxiety will become very anxious when asked to perform or participate in a particular activity that will trigger anxiety, such as feeling suddenly weak when asked to speak or stammering when asked to speak.

Similarly, the feelings of anxiety for both types of social anxiety include getting worried a lot about embarrassing oneself in front of people and feeling highly anxious before getting into any social context. One will be spent efforts trying to anticipate all embarrassing things that can happen in a public situation. In all forms of anxiety, the individual lacks the willpower to speak their mind. The person will reflect continuously on the alternatives that he or she could have taken.

Relatedly, social anxiety will also manifest in physical signs and symptoms, including having a dry mouth, sweating, heart pounding, wanting to use washrooms, heartbeats that are irregular, and feelings of numbness in the fingers. Some of the other visible signs of social anxiety include stammering, blushing, trembling, and shaking. All these symptoms can be distressing and aggravate anxiety. Sometimes, one may worry a lot to the extent of exhibiting a worried look. A significant number of people affected by social anxiety tend to align their lives around their symptoms of social anxiety.

In particular, such an individual has to contend with missing out on things they might otherwise participate in and enjoy. For instance, if one is affected by social anxiety, he or she may not visit a friend, concert, or go shopping. Some people avoid taking a promotion at work even though they merit it. A significant number of people with social anxiety have challenges in building and maintaining long-term relationships. The other people with a high risk for social anxiety include those with high expectations for their behavior in public and those who have stammered as a child.

Furthermore, what makes social anxiety sustainable are certain thoughts that activate when one enters a social situation and makes the person anxious. Some of these thoughts include reflecting and activating rules for oneself, beliefs about oneself, and making predictions. These thoughts make one think and criticize their behavior from moment to moment. For individuals with social anxiety, such thoughts are automatic and seem to project the true inner self of the afflicted person. For instance, these thoughts make one imagine that they appear to other people in a specific manner, which is usually unattractive.

Unfortunately, people with social anxiety will engage in safety behaviors that make them feel they are in more control of the social situation. The specific behaviors include drinking alcohol, shunning eye contact, avoiding speaking about oneself, and asking the other person too many questions. The counterproductive aspect of these safety behaviors is that they deny one the opportunity to face their fears as their anxiety is masked.

What is not social anxiety?

First, imposter syndrome is not social anxiety. The imposter syndrome is an unjustified feeling of fear that one is not as competent as he or she appears. People with the imposter syndrome set a ridiculously high-performance bar for themselves, and when they do not attain that high mark, they feel they are a fraud, a letdown, and not worthy of their current position. As a way of compensating, a person with imposter syndrome will avoid people where possible because they are always under the impression that people will find out that they are a fraud. If unmanaged, the imposter syndrome will manifest not as social anxiety but as a secondary condition.

Second, fear is not necessarily social anxiety. For instance, if one fears a social event will embarrass the person and that feeling is short-lived or occasional, it does not qualify as social anxiety. There are some events and occasions that can heighten one's fear in social settings. For instance, post-trauma can manifest as social anxiety, especially where the initial traumatizing event happened within a public space. Then there are feelings of shame that can make one avoid certain places and people, but usually this is short-lived. Social anxiety arises where the fear and uneasiness of engaging in social interactions are unjustified and chronic, and overwhelming the affected person.

Self-Assessment Social Anxiety Test

Suppose you feel worried and panicked in social interactions or just the thought of being in them. In that case, the following social anxiety assessment can help ascertain if you meet the diagnostic criteria for social anxiety. Research the location of the test or ask your therapist.

Chapter 5:
Environmental Decluttering

H uman beings are hardwired for personal connections because our relationships complete us and fill the void. This is one reason why we are always looking to form fruitful relationships. However, most of the time, the relationships we form become a burden. We are not able to sustain them or feel constrained by them. The inability to sustain relationships has become a widespread phenomenon for some time. It can lead to unhappiness, discontent, and mental fatigue.

It is important to understand that relationships are two-way connections. Unrealistic expectations in relationships contribute to the problem. It isn't the other partner in the relationship that causes the friction, but your expectations of the partner. If you are expecting something from your partner, you may become disappointed. Even setting rules doesn't help as it is not a matter of receiving but perception.

Expectations from any relationship can cloud the thinking process. You are receiving mode and start quantifying the unquantifiable. As a result, mutual trust and respect start fading. You become more and more demanding and less forgiving and accepting. Each and everything keep getting registered in your mind and clutters it. Of note, the reactions arising in such cases are spontaneous.

If you want to have healthy relationships, then being instinctive should be shunned. Mindfulness is the only way to cultivate nourishing relationships. You cannot let your mind become cluttered and prejudices rule your relationships. The clutter in your mind will make you unreceptive and unjustified. It will inflate your ego and make you unkind and uncompassionate.

Maintaining a relationship with another human being is a tightrope walk. You may be dealing with someone with the same level of intellect but a completely different set of problems. You may be living in the same home, working the same type of jobs, and having the same circle of friends, yet your worlds can be completely different. Every person has a unique perception of things, and individuals have their way of quantifying problems. Every person has unique triggers of stress and joy. Measuring the other person with the same yardstick will create problems. The bigger problem is if you have a cluttered mind and never come to understand the things that cause friction.

The best way to cultivate nourishing relationships is to declutter your mind, become more mindful, and eliminate your prejudices.

Be More Inclusive

Humans considers themselves to be the most intelligent race on this earth. They have the power to understand and rationalize. It may be accurate to a great extent when it comes to an understanding other organisms and systems, and it may also work in understanding your partner.

Another human being is also as complex as you. Trying to understand the other person all the time is a strategy doomed to fail. You can never accurately predict another person's circumstances, outlook, and reactions in a situation. The more you try to understand the person, the more alarm and defensiveness you'll cause. Relationships are not about accurately understanding but about being inclusive. It would help if you accepted your partners with all their merits and demerits. It is the only way to disarm them to let their guard down. The harder you try to understand, the tougher the situation will get.

Listen

Most of the problems in a relationship need better listening. When you are listening without judging, you are giving vent to the problems of your partner. This helps in accepting their problems and giving them a chance to open up. It increases the bond and releases stress. Your attentiveness is all your partner seeks most of the time. Most people can solve their problems, and if they need you, they'll ask for your help. You only need to pay attention to the things they want to get off their chest.

Mind Your Words

Opinions are double-edged swords in a relationship. If you are not mindful of the things you say, your relationship can go south. One of the biggest problems in sour relationships is speaking unmindfully. People do not pay attention to the things they say and do not foresee the extent of damage they can cause. Your opinions are only good for you. Do not push them on your partner, or it can easily become worse than a prime-time TV debate. Mindful speaking is the only way to keep the guard of your partner down.

Don't Pick and Choose the Qualities

The main difference between human beings and robots is that every individual comes with a unique set of qualities. You can make any number of robots with identical qualities and features. We may like it or not, but this is a truth we need to accept. Nothing harms a relationship more than selective picking the qualities in a person. It raises their guard and makes them defensive and skeptical. Comparing of two individuals is inhuman. A person with a set of qualities comes with a separate set of vices. If your mind is cluttered, you will not be able to see this. Selective viewing can endanger any relationship.

You must understand that relationships are not absolute. There will always be variables, and they need mindful adjustments. They will need your careful attention. They will need your acceptance. Decluttering your mind is very important in making you more receptive. It enables you to pay attention to the important things.

Getting into a relationship is fairly easy as attraction is the key here. Two individuals can become close due to attraction, where only your strong points matter. You are displaying your strengths and passing on your apparent merit. However, maintaining a relationship is a completely different ball game. You cannot pretend to be your best all the time. You cannot pretend anything at all. All your flaws will become obvious, and the same goes for your partner. If you are not inclusive in your approach, the relationship will fall apart sooner than later.

To accept so many things in your partner and still be reasonably satisfied, your mind must be receptive. A cluttered mind will fail you here. You will either end up pretending to accept or falter. In both instances, things wouldn't end pleasantly for you. On the other hand, mindfulness ensures that you are in a ready state to accept the facts. You can take the facts as they are and live with them. This will ensure that your partner feels more welcomed and comfortable. Therefore, decluttering your mind is an essential step towards building lasting relationships that can work for you. These relationships will bring joy and happiness to your life. You wouldn't feel suffocated, and there will be no danger of them turning toxic.

How do You Use Affirmations to Declutter Your Mind?

Affirmations are consciously formatted positive statements frequently said (either aloud or in written form) with the intent of positively influencing a person's thoughts and actions. The statements are aimed at impacting an individual's conscious as well as subconscious mind.

Affirmations are highly potent tools for changing a person's mood, altering his state of mind, manifesting change, and getting what you yearn for in life. However, affirmations work more effectively when a person can identify a belief that is holding them back or cluttering their mind.

Affirmations are designed to activate the power of your subconscious mind. They motivate you and keep your mind focused on the bigger picture or goals. Affirmations can alter the way you think, feel, and behave. Positive statements help you stay more mentally active, enthusiastic, and positive. They inspire and energize you to make better decisions and be the best version of yourself. Affirmations help eliminate negative mental clutter and chaos by focusing on the positives and thus being led into doing more thinking of more positive, focused, and clear thoughts daily.

Affirmations should be simple, short, and easy to remember. Think about this. You are on your way back home from the office and stuck in a lot of traffic. You have some time to go through your affirmations while you are still there doing nothing. Hey, the only jinx is that you can't remember or recall it since it was so elaborate and long. There, you now have a valid excuse for not using affirmations. Short and simple affirmations work best because you can easily keep saying them without forgetting the words or having to refer to your notes to gather the exact words.

Start by creating a list of affirmations that resonate with you, and represent what you want in life in the best possible manner. It doesn't have to be something grand or ambitious. Your affirmation can be something as basic as "peace of mind and happiness." Keep it so that it instantly rings a bell with you. Use statements that you connect with on a deeper level. While there's no hard and fast rule about when or how to say these positive statements, I'd highly recommend setting aside a special time or ritual for them.

When we are asleep, we are essentially resting our conscious mind and putting our subconscious to work. This means anything we feed our subconscious mind just before its activity peaks has a greater chance of being absorbed and retained. Similarly, affirmations prove to be more effective when the subconscious mind is in a more receptive state during meditation or mindfulness.

Create affirmations you can identify with. Your affirmations should be in complete alignment with individual goals, dreams, objectives, and visions. What is it that truly matters to you? Whom do you want to become? What is your ultimate goal in life? How do you want to live your life?

Your affirmations should reflect the ideal you want to accomplish in life. For instance, a more successful and rewarding career, a happy home, an understanding partner, and healthy, happy children listen to you. Please don't copy and paste someone else's affirmations and apply them to your life. Your affirmations should scream from you all the way. Keep it something you instantly identify with.

Affirmations should always use positive words and phrases. Sometimes, I've had people coming up to me and telling me they keep saying their affirmations several times throughout the day and yet have no visible results. Don't focus on what you don't want. Instead, talk only about what you want.

Talk about it as if happening in the present. Your subconscious and the universe should be led to believe that it is your reality and not something you aspire to. If you aspire to have more mental clarity and peace, don't say, "I am going to accomplish more mental peace and clarity." Rather say, "I am mentally at peace and have complete clarity about my life."

Talking about something as if you want it in the future reinforces the lack of it in your present. If you say you will be mentally at peace in the future, it simply means you are not at peace currently. And reinforcing a lack of something attracts more of the lack of it. So, saying something that denotes a lack of mental peace will only attract more of this lack of mental peace. Talk about the positives or goals as if you already have them or have accomplished them.

Repetition is the key to allowing your subconscious to take aboard what you want to accomplish. Fill them with compelling emotions. The more emotions you infuse into your positive statements or affirmations, the most effective results you are likely to accomplish. Don't simply say your affirmations clinically because some self-help coach goaded you into it. It is an utterly pointless practice.

Feel them as you say them. Feel excited and energized by the affirmations. Live your affirmations. Allow yourself to be completely taken over by them. Get into the habit of measuring/tracking results. Make a note of things that have changed for the better in your life after you started saying these affirmations. This will prevent you from saying them more mechanically and make you even more excited about using them.

Affirmations can also be what you have or are rather than what you want to be. While we are always focusing on things we want to achieve, we seldom pay attention to the positives we already possess. Human beings are constantly dwelling on elements they'd rather change about themselves or their lives.

However, breaking this pattern and affirming what you truly appreciate about yourself awards you with the required confidence to change the not so amazing things about yourself. This way, you learn to accept great things about yourself and gain the confidence to be what you want to be in the future. Make a list of all your positive attributes. Write them down in a manner where you can spot them every day.

Visualize your future or affirmations (as you'd like them to be). While visualizing, keep repeating your affirmations. Think carefully about what every word you are uttering means. Think about its impact on your present and future. Feel every word entering the realm of your subconscious mind and influencing your behavior, and ultimately your life. Feel your mind clearing up to occupy thoughts related to these affirmations. Pay careful attention to what every word means and implies in your life.

Chapter 6:

Body and Mind

Whenever you want control within the mind and body, you want to consider the recent technologies on the planet. You can ascertain exactly what you want to accomplish in terms of personal empowerment. You shouldn't be overly concerned about finding methods to get there. Although brain programming is real, and we all experience it to some extent, there are many opportunities to adjust or even change our default program.

With the expansion of science around the world, a growing number of scientists from different clinical fields have found that a slight proportion of our brain is employed. They agree that our brains have a much higher level of consciousness and we might even know how to get there.

Connected not related

The body and mind problem concerns their difference. Your brain is all about the psychological dimension, awareness, and thought. Your body is all about physiology as impacted by brain impulses. Humans are material beings with weight and solidity, and containing various fluids. Contrary to inanimate elements (e.g., stones), humans have produced a rationale for their presence. In short, we have "brains".

Traditionally, people are distinguished by having a mind (non-physical) and a body/brain (physical). That is referred to as dualism, the belief that the body and mind exist as separate entities. Rene

Descartes' dualism asserted that there's a two-way relationship between our physical and mental compounds. He set the groundwork for the later theories of the mind-body issue. The mind-body problem is among those most contentious issues today, causing passionate debate among contemporary philosophers, such as Colin McGinn, who genuinely believes the problem is so ironic that people will never have the ability to solve it. Man will never hold the concepts necessary to comprehend how consciousness emerges from a material platform.

So separate or intertwined, how can a soggy gray mass such as the brain contribute to the extraordinary phenomenon of awareness? The digital revolution has provided the impetus to probe the matter further well beyond Descartes. The typical reply to the question is a uniquely modern variant of Descartes. Descartes is like the first bible in pronouncing a modern idea of comprehension and mental performance. Undoubtedly Descartes' dualism ignited an enormous argument in the century that followed his novel theory. The argument might have gone underground occasionally; however, in one form or the other, it appears in the present.

But there is a gap between then and now. Descartes and other philosophers of his time were concerned with theological problems. The mind-body problem wasn't a freestanding, academic issue; it was bound up with the concept of immortality. Descartes thought he could sell his doctrine to the Catholic Church and provide a stable foundation for the Christian philosophy of immortality. Materialism eventually would undermine this philosophy.

The associated issue of individuality has a similar history. Few philosophical issues are as engaging to students as what makes someone an individual. The first recognizable modern formulation of the challenge is found in Locke's essay Concerning Human Understanding. The focus shifted immensely from the Cartesian soul to materialism, a philosophy underlining much of modern science.

The issue of private individuality now extrapolates from recent advancements in biomedical technology. Locke's basic motivation, of course was rather different from the philosophers of today. Locke questioned the body's ability to survive death in any form. Much like Descartes, he worried about the views of the church - in his instance the Anglican church. Today it is not particularly relevant and science reigns supreme. It is still a Janus-faced era that has provoked considerable concern and research.

Why Exercising is Crucial

Everyone knows that exercising your body is a significant goal that affords great advantages. But exercising the mind is every bit as crucial - not just to benefit your own body but also to keep the mind functioning at a high stage. It helps ward off afflictions of the mind, like memory loss, and Alzheimer's disease in all age groups. Even though there aren't any medications to stop mental decline, you can you can perform exercises to keep the mind sharp and attentive.

Add healthy eating and avoiding practices that harm the cells, such as smoking. Staying occupied and happy is a great antidote to depression and overeating. We all have conscious thoughts, and we go to sleep contemplating all sorts of matters. In short, we allow random thoughts to dominate our minds.

The mind tends to wander and get overloaded with politics, and societal, economic, community and individual troubles, even spiritual concerns. Staving off mental issues requires forcing your mind to engage in a high level of activity. You need to take part in stimulating mental activities to fortify the brain tissues and neural links. Don't go for long spans without extending, stretching, and pushing your mind to take on fresh, new challenges and react to stimulation.

Enrolling in continuing education classes or going for an advanced degree are good ways to exercise the mind. You're made to study, remember new material, and to multi-task. You can join a reading group, engage in online forums or do any other mental activity you like. The point is to exercise both the body and the mind.

There is no known cure for Alzheimer's disease that gradually destroys the individual's memory and ability to know, reason, make judgments, communicate and carry out daily tasks. It progressively destroys brain cells and ultimately proves fatal.

By stimulating the mind, you can to drive back the pathologies linked to the illness. Crossword or sudoku puzzles, reading novels, or learning a new language, just do anything to excite mental performance. You will find other brain learning methods to assist mental performance on both the left and right hemispheres. The scientific world has long proven that the left hemisphere deals with reason and logic. By contrast, the right hemisphere is in charge of the creative and aesthetic realm. Einstein used this left-right synergy in devising his famous formula, $e=mc2$. Special mind thoughts or

 training methods have grown in the previous century and especially the previous decades. Individuals are known to possess incredible feats of memory such as linking hundreds of faces and names, long arithmetic formulas in addition to long strings of numbers. Some practical software is offered to provide your head with a workout. It can slow (not cure) Alzheimer's illness. Such methods are extremely simple to learn and are formerly used, remaining with all of our lives, allowing the mind to store huge amounts of information employed at school, work, or during an everyday activity.

But the majority of men and women begin their lives without even knowing that such terrific methods are readily available. As a person gets older, the mind becomes fuzzier. There's a tendency to forget things, names, and places. There's the terrifying potential of developing Alzheimer's illness. Pros advise people 40 and above to exercise their minds consistently. Mental performance shouldn't be stagnant. Reading would be the ideal solution to keeping the human brain occupied. It's possible to read not merely novels and articles, but whatever comes your way like a real estate booklet, insurance coverage, an external advertisement, a solicitation letter.

Watching television or movies can be a mind practice, particularly if there is a whodunit storyline. You have to analyze the scenario and use your brain. Game shows such as Jeopardy and Wheel of Fortune feed your brain while you put yourself in the shoes of the contestants.

Computers provide additional help. There are many word games and assorted puzzles on the internet that need analytical competency. You might even surf the net to acquire new information on any topic. You could be busy on Facebook or Twitter and increase your range of friends. All of the above are fun. These won't simply exercise the mind but will also assist in passing the time.

History shows us that men and women who develop an art or have a fantastic scientific breakthrough are tremendously creative.

Therefore, we must spend more hours developing our mental intelligence and get all these creative juices flowing. According to oriental medicine, those who spend too long overthinking end up having health issues. They aren't functioning properly and therefore are unbalanced in mind and body. Most of us know individuals who overanalyze a circumstance and suffer from poor digestion and associated issues. Stress contributes to gut ulcers. Exactly how many physiatrists find themselves being patients?

But isn't thinking a learned response? We remember our responses to various situations. We realize how we have to respond if a problem arises. The simple fact is that we utilize between 5 and 3% of our brains, so what's the remainder doing? Nobody knows for certain, aside from something to do with the subconscious, also called our intuition. Whenever we need to make a quick choice, we utilize our intuitive abilities. We dismiss our instincts and become less creative when we overthink. We make conclusions based on memories and knowledge, understanding that we regurgitating old memories.

Our thought patterns might be negative, upsetting, and limiting. Many people compare believing something to some sort of crutch, similar to smoking. Thinking too difficult saves us from needing to come to such a choice. But it isn't the best solution after all.

Chapter 7:

How to Declutter Your Mind

U nreturned calls, unanswered emails, uncompleted tasks on your computer, work papers cluttering all over your desk, unused items and clothes, a messy apartment, pressure from your workplace, an unreasonable boss, and piled up bills – these are few examples of the clutter that can cause stress and anxiety in your life.

The harder you force things and stop new clutter in your life, the more you will feel stressed, pressured, anxious, and overwhelmed. Clutter is a cruel cycle that holds you back from living the life you want. Fortunately, there's a way to get your life back. By understanding the effects of clutter and taking the right steps to declutter, you can begin to live a stress-free life and escape anxiety.

So, let's get started with the changes you need to make.

Anger Management

Pressure, stress, anticipation, and other issues can trigger emotions. As a peak performer, you need to control your emotions before your emotions take full control. Anger clouds your judgment and causes a lack of productivity if not managed properly. Below are ways to manage your anger, change the bad habit, and improve your performance.

It is important to realize that anger is a problem and that affects the well-being of the mind and it must be addressed with management.

Who are you angry at? You need to understand if you are angry at yourself, your environment, your job, or at other people.

By understanding your anger, you come to identify what sets it off and the people that trigger your mood. Record the times when you react explosively or impulsively in your "anger journal book." You will understand what anger feels like and what it is doing to you. Begin by asking ourselves questions like:

- Who does my anger affect?
- Why is anger my problem?
- What are the things I say or do when I'm angry?
- What are my reactions to anger? – Do I get physical? Do I get violent? Do I grit my teeth, clench my fists, or even punch or throw things around?
- Do I get a burning sensation in my stomach or my throat when I'm angry?
- How do I feel when I get angry?

Once we identify our triggers and know exactly how we react, we can start to understand the root causes of our anger. Is our anger a personality flaw? Is it due to insecurity? Is it because of pressure? And so on. After we sort out all the details, we can control our anger issues.

Channel Your Emotions and Let it Out

One of the first suggestions you will get when it comes to anger is to let your emotions out and not bottle them up. It is true. Giving your emotions an outlet brings relief. An outlet to your emotions could be anything that helps you release those pent-up emotions. It could be walking around the block when you are ticked off instead of reacting. If going to the gym to life some heavy weights or beating a bag up is your outlet, then go right ahead! If you feel writing or reading helps free your mind, collect your thoughts, organize and maintain control, go and do it! Anything you find comfortable as an outlet instead of acting impulsively is ideal.

The aim of letting your emotions out is to channel all that energy you would have wasted in an outburst into something productive and useful in the future. Find ways to let your emotions out instead of bottling them. There is a more positive way to express your emotions, be it through hobbies or other activities you find interesting.

Deep Breath. Just Breathe

One of the quickest ways to calm the body is through deep, slow breathing. New research suggests that this keeps neurons in the brain from signaling the arousal center in your body so you can avoid getting worked up.

Count Numbers

The conscious, rational mind moves much slower than the subconscious mind, which is responsible for the flight-or-flight response, so give it some time to catch up. Counting from 1 – 10 or 10 – 1 helps cool the innate adrenaline response. Your body will, in turn, release certain hormones to balance your body and help reduce impulsive actions.

Always Think Twice and Even Trice Before Reacting

Although this sounds easy, it is always harder when putting it into practice, especially when you are getting worked up or reacting. You need to pause and think about your current activities and see if it is worth it. Try thinking fond thoughts and recall good memories and see if it helps. You can also employ your breathing exercise at this point to help you stay calm.

Vent

At times, we just need to let it all out and talk about how we are feeling, why we are angry or upset, and how we feel wronged. If you have a confidant to vent to, then go right ahead! They just have to listen and not respond or try to help. Having someone listen helps get most of the things bothering us off our chests and gets rid of some of the things weighing on our minds. Venting helps us get a better perspective on our emotions when we hear ourselves out loud.

Locate the Humor in Your Anger

This technique is somewhat underused, but it is quite helpful in diffusing a state of anger. It is very effective, especially when dealing with people who annoy and make you angry. For instance, if someone makes fun of you or insults you, hoping to get you all worked up, instead of blowing all hot to the insult, which could further escalate the situation and maybe end in violence, you could use self-deprecating humor. Let's take a look at a few examples.

Example 1:

A colleague: "You look terrible in that silly outfit."

Me: "If you say this outfit is silly, then you should have seen the one I initially wanted to wear."

Example 2:

A friend: "I keep wondering what you are good at."

Me: "That's how helpful I am."

Responding in similar ways will disarm those who make unsolicited or rude remarks about you. When people talk or behave in ways that would anger me, I would rather diffuse the situation by disarming them with self-deprecating humor instead of escalating the whole situation.

Avoid Things That Trigger You

The way we react to people and different situations cannot always be controlled. There are times when some things or people just become so annoying and get on our nerves. Usually, such situations will lead to a total blow-up. This can be even more difficult when we are just starting to manage and control our anger. It would be wiser and easier if you could completely avoid triggers.

If reading tweets makes you angry, then just delete your account or simply uninstall the App. If driving during the rush hour periods drives you mad or gives you road rage, just find a way to get to your destination earlier or later when the rush hour period is over.

As long as you can afford to make changes that will make you happier, just go ahead and make them. On a final note, if you feel your anger is out of control and you can no longer manage it, get help. If it leads to violence and affects your life on a general level, affecting your relationships and interfering with your work, seek help by talking to your doctor.

Stop Overthinking

On the surface, overthinking seems harmless and doesn't sound bad at all – after all, thinking is a good thing, right? The truth is that overthinking can cause serious health problems. It can cause your judgments to become clouded and elevate your level of your stress. Spending too much time on negative thoughts will impair your ability to act. If you feel this is familiar terrain, let's discuss some important ways to stop or avoid overthinking.

Distract Yourself into Happiness

One of the simplest but effective methods to stop overthinking is by distracting yourself with happy and positive thoughts and activities, as healthy alternatives to negative emotions. Activities like dancing, sports/exercise, meditation, drawing/painting, or playing an instrument can create the required distraction, enough for you to overcome and shut down overthinking.

Awareness is the Road to Change

This step is a universal one to address the issue of overthinking. If you are not aware of when overthinking occurs in your mind, find a way to identify it and then distract yourself. Therefore, whenever you start feeling stress, self-doubt, or anxiety, you take a step back and take a closer look at the situation. In your moment of awareness, you will find the right road to the change you desire.

Think of What Can go Right Instead of What Can go Wrong

Fear is the main emotion that causes overthinking. When you focus too much on the negative, thinking of the things that might happen, you easily become paralyzed with fear. Whenever you notice that you are leaning in that direction, STOP. Start visualizing all the things that remain in your positive zone. Negative emotions can cause a lack of motivation that affects your overall performance.

Don't Wait for Perfection

It is good to be ambitious, but trying to reach perfection is impractical, unrealistic, and draining. Every single thing need not be perfect. Of course not. Doing your best is quite good, but it is another thing entirely to try too hard on every little detail. Doing so is not good for your mental health as it can propel you into a state of anxiety, paralysis, and of course lead to procrastination.

We need to stop waiting for perfection and begin to progress. When you start thinking that some things need to be perfect before you are satisfied, you should a remind yourself that it is not a smart move to wait for perfection. You need to start making progress and stop overthinking "perfection."

Put Things into Perspective

It is easier to destroy than to create; the same goes for blowing things out of proportion and falling into negative emotions. When you sense you are making a big deal out of nothing or your actions are destructive more than creative, take a step back and put things into perspective. Ask yourself if it will matter much a few years from now, or even a few months from now. Switching the timeframe with can help you stop overthinking.

Change Your View of Fear

Whether you are afraid of trying because of the unknown or fearful because you have failed in the past, know that just because things didn't work out in the past doesn't means it won't work out if you try again. It would help if you changed how you view fear. Remember that every new opportunity is also a new beginning and you have a new starting point.

Put a Timer to Work

Give yourself a time limit. We are humans, and we have emotions. If you need to worry, set your timer to 10 minutes, and use that time to think and analyze all the things in your mind. Once you have exhausted the 10 minutes and your timer goes off, set another 10 minutes. Then get your pen and paper and write down the things causing you anxiety, worry, and stress. After the 10-minute timer goes off, rip up the paper and move to something positive and more fun.

Live in The Moment: You Can't Predict the Future

All we have is this moment because no one can predict the future. If you spend all your present time worrying and thinking about the future, you are only depriving yourself of the present reality. It is not productive to spend all your time worrying about a future yet to come. Your time is valuable, so spend it on things that make you happy and bring joy.

You can also practice mindfulness to build self-esteem. Right now, mindfulness-based cognitive behavior therapy (MBCT) is very popular, and it helps stop overthinking. It can help you understand the relationship between your feelings and your way of thinking.

Accept Your Best

Feeling you are not good enough can affect your peak performance, cause overthinking, and impair your general health. Accepting your best will save you from those sleepless nights of feeling down, thinking you are not dedicated or hardworking enough. Therefore, you are never good enough. Once you embark on any endeavor and have given it your best effort, accept it and know that there are some things you can't control. You have done all that you could do.

Be Grateful

If you seem to be feeling grateful or regretful, you can't be both at the same time. So, spend time being grateful and positive. You can make a list of the things you are grateful for. You can even make a gratitude friend and talk about it or exchange lists, so someone else knows what you are grateful for.

No one is immune to overthinking, and it can happen to anyone. But if you have a means for protecting yourself from overthinking, you can avoid unnecessary stress, anxiety, or negative emotions. You can be more productive, effective, and positive in several aspects of your life. Here is more on how to do it.

Mental Toughness

A unique characteristic of great athletes is their ability to remain focused and able to consistently perform well under pressure. These athletes do allow the expectations or pressure of fans, coaches, teammates, and opponents to unsettle them. It is because of their "mental toughness." Mental strength and toughness help performers to flourish under extreme and competitive situations. As a performer, you need to build and upgrade your mental toughness to elevate your performance. Let's take a look at some of the ways we can build mental strength.

Skill Acquisition

The process of acquiring a new skillset can help in building mental toughness. You will develop a mastery over the skill and a sense of competency, both of which are crucial and can be utilized under pressure or during challenging times. In short, they will boost your problem-solving ability and self-esteem.

The type of skill you choose to learn will depend on your individual preference. Some people gain a benefit when they learn new hobbies and challenging games through competency-based learning. Others might benefit from improving their cognitive skills, such as working their memories through visualizing or selective attention, while improving their daily functioning. When you acquire skills in a group setting, you gain the added benefit of social support, which will also boost your mental toughness and resilience.

Goal Setting

Developing goals and learning the steps to accomplish these goals can build willpower and mental toughness. Goals can be almost anything, big or small, and they can be related to education, spirituality, physical health, career, emotions, finance, and a lot more. Meanwhile, goals that involve skill acquisition usually have double benefits because you gain the skill and build mental toughness at the same time. For example, learning how to speak a new language or how to play the piano.

Controlled Exposure

Controlled exposure is when you are carefully and gradually exposed to anxiety-provoking situations to help you overcome your fears. Research suggests that it can improve mental toughness, especially when related to goal setting or skill acquisition. In fact, you get a triple benefit.

Let's take public speaking, a very useful life skill. Many people dread it because it evokes fear. People who dread public speaking can overcome their fears, set goals, acquire the skill through controlled exposure. They start by gradually exposing themselves to a small audience of about one or two people, then gradually and continuously increase the size of the audience over time.

This controlled exposure strategy can be self-tutored, or it can be initiated and with a trained therapist in Cognitive Behavioral Therapy. Should the process be successful, you can apply it during any adversity since you will gain a sense of autonomy and increased self-esteem.

Stop Seeing Crises as Impossible Problems

We can do little to nothing to stop problems, nor can we change the external events happening around us. But we can control how we react to these events. Life comes with different challenges, but what is more important is to look beyond all those challenges in any stressful situation you find yourself in. Remember that all circumstances change with time.

Change is a Part of Living

They say nothing is permanent in life, and change is constant. Consequently, you face difficult circumstances, but what is important to know is when certain goals are no longer attainable or realistic. Accepting change is part of living, and that there are certain things you don't have control over. You should focus on what matters. Over time, your mental toughness will get firmer.

Take Care of Yourself

An essential strategy for building mental toughness is caring for yourself. Self-care keeps your mind and your body at an optimum state to deal with difficult situations and circumstances should they arise. By taking care of yourself, you attend to your personal feelings and needs. You can get involved in activities that helps you relax and bring you joy. Self-care also involves regular physical exercise.

Meditation and Visualization

Practicing meditation and visualization greatly helps build mental toughness, especially if your job requires major mental, emotional, and physical inputs while on the job, such as soldiers, police officers, firefighters, and other first responders.

Visualization can help you visualize how a task should be done; that way, your resolve can be strengthened. It prepares your mind and entire being for real action. When the actual time for performance arrives, you have already done that thing over and over probably hundreds of times, and you will be mentally and physically prepared.

Meditation strengthens our inner being and sharpens the mind and body ahead of tasks. It helps focus the mind, eliminate fear, instill confidence, calm down, and become more calculative, boosting our motivation and cranking up our mental toughness.

Take Decisive Action

Don't shy away from challenges that seem stressful and problematic; you can't hide or wish them away. You need to take decisive action whenever possible. You will start building the mindset of a performer, and your mental fortitude will also change for the better.

Yoga and Meditation

Your boss is talking to you while your mobile phone is ringing. You managed to see your partner's name on the screen. While you are trying to concentrate on what your boss is saying, you are also wondering why your partner is calling you. Is it an emergency or something has happened? Stress and anxiety are everywhere, and this makes us lose concentration and perform less than expected. If stress is getting the best of you, now is the time to take your mat and try out yoga and meditate.

Yoga and Meditation Reduce Anxiety

Yoga is a mind and body practice that involves physical poses, relaxation, controlled breathing, and meditation. Yoga can greatly reduce stress and lower your heart rate. The good thing about yoga is that it is simple, and anyone can do it.

Yoga has gained popularity over the years, thanks to its benefit in renewing the body by enhancing flexibility, balance, and strength. Anxiety disorders have a lot of uncomfortable symptoms such as tension and pain sensitivity. With yoga postures, you can release the muscle tension all over the body.

These yoga poses are taught in a particular order. It also helps to control anxious thoughts. Frequent worries and negative thinking patterns are common symptoms of anxiety. Meditation and focusing on the breath help a lot in letting go. Generally, practicing yoga will impart a relaxation response, allowing the mind and body to enjoy a sense of ease and calm.

Many people have the misconception that meditation works like magic, and it can automatically reduce anxiety. The main purpose of meditation is not to banish anxiety; instead, it is to help you be present in every moment. Reducing anxiety is a side effect of its primary purpose. The major reason why we experience anxiety is that we worry too much about the past or future. When we meditate, we are intentionally focusing on the "now."

Meditation helps to reduce anxiety because it calms an overactive brain. People with anxiety often feel as if their mind is a hamster on a wheel "always running and not getting anywhere." We start feeling anxious as we buy into our feelings and thoughts. We get overwhelmed with these thoughts, and yet they aren't worth our attention. With meditation, you will stop overthinking and limit the unnecessary attention we give to random but overwhelming thoughts. Meditation gets us off the wheel to catch our breath and gain a better perspective.

To practice basic meditation, you need to focus on your breath and pay attention to the sensation of your breathing. If your mind wanders, don't worry; gently guide it back to your breath. You can use your breath as a focal point by bringing your attention to the present instead of allowing distractions to take your attention away.

Over time and with constant practice, your attention will be strengthened. You will get good at paying attention and not "running on the mental hamster wheel." To see real results, be patient and consistent. You might not see much difference in the beginning, but with commitment, you will get results. Finally, meditation helps us slow down, and this makes us less anxious. All in all, you can enhance your mood, rewire your brain, and ease your anxiety with meditation and yoga techniques.

Take Note of How You Feel Emotionally, Mentally, and Physically

Start by placing one hand on your chest and the other hand on your belly. Exhale completely and count downwards, from 5 to 1. Inhale into your hand on your chest and count to 5. Again, exhale and count backward from 5. Inhale again and count to 5, and exhale as you count from 5. Now, inhale into the hand on your belly and count 5 seconds, exhale, and count from 5. Repeat these ten times, and you will feel better after.

Take a Walk and Match Your Stride to Your Breath

As you take a walk, take note of the smells and sounds around you. Take note of the temperature on your skin. If possible, step on the ground with your bare feet. This technique is referred to as grounding, and it is a very powerful tool when you start feeling anxiety setting in.

Practice Sun Salutations

While standing or seated, take a few mini sun salutations. You do this by inhaling while reaching both of your arms up over your head and exhaling while connecting your palms over your heart space. Repeat by inhaling as you look up, exhale through and release your hands towards the mat. After this, pause and take a few breaths as you press your hands on your mat. Soften your shoulders and slow down your breathing. Repeat this exercise 3 to 5 times.

Legs Up the Wall Pose?

For those times when anxiety is manifesting, maybe with jittery legs, try taking the legs up the wall pose. This pose is also called the "Viparita Karani" in Sanskrit. Start by lying down on the floor after finding a wall space to use. Now, bring your legs to the wall and create a 90-degree angle with it and your upper body. Next, shimmy your shoulders underneath you while pressing the back of your head into the ground and breathe gently. This leg up the wall pose can be done anywhere, and it's for everybody, especially people who have stress.

Be Mindful of What You Consume

Loud music, excessive screen time, caffeine, and sugar greatly contribute to an anxious mind. You can focus on incorporating calmer things like a relaxation bath, a silent meditation, or a walk-in nature. Instead of consuming too much caffeine, switch to tea. If you consume a lot of sugar, try incorporating sweets with a low-glycemic index, containing whole-fruit or coconut sugar.

Nutrition and Exercise

Research suggests that certain foods contribute to an increased level of anxiety. These foods can have a great impact on people with an anxiety disorder by intensifying the physical symptoms. This prevents you from getting a good night's rest and increases your rate of panic attacks.

A common dietary anxiety trigger is caffeine. Many of us start our days with coffee as it helps us to feel alert and energized. However, it has been found that caffeine triggers panic attacks and increases feelings of irritability and nervousness. Caffeine is also known to cause other physical symptoms like shaking and trembling, which is very common among people with anxiety disorders. Even for people who don't have the disorder, caffeine is still associated with increased anxiety.

The negative effects of caffeine will make you want to take it off your diet immediately. On a side note, if you are already considering taking caffeine off your diet or reducing it, do it gradually. Eliminating it abruptly may cause withdrawal symptoms like restlessness, headaches, and irritability. Note that caffeine isn't found in just coffee; it can also be found in tea, chocolate, and sodas. Sugar and alcohol have also been found to impair our moods and feelings. They may cause low energy levels, sleep disturbances, and nervousness. Monosodium Glutamate (MSG) is a food additive used to enhance flavor that has side effects like dizziness, sweating, nausea, and in some cases a panic attack.

Some foods to reduce anxiety:

- Foods rich in zinc like cashews, oysters, beef, liver, and egg yolks.
- Diets high in magnesium such as Swiss chard, spinach, nuts, legumes, seeds, nuts, and whole grains.

- Probiotic food like pickles, kefir, and pickles.
- Fatty fish like wild Alaskan salmon containing omega-3 fatty acids.
- Foods rich in Vitamin B. Examples are almonds and avocado.
- Asparagus

Should Antioxidants be Included in Your Anti-Anxiety Diet?

Anxiety has been said to be connected with a lowered antioxidant state. Therefore, it is reasonable that improving your diet with foods that contain a lot of antioxidants may help relieve the symptoms of anxiety disorders. Antioxidant-rich foods, herbs, spices, beverages, and supplements include:

- Fruits: prunes, apples (Granny Smith, Gala, Red Delicious), plums, and sweet cherries
- Beans: Pinto, dried small red, black, red kidney
- Nuts: pecans, walnuts
- Berries: strawberries, blackberries, blueberries, cranberries, raspberries
- Vegetables: kale, artichokes, spinach, broccoli, beets
- Spices containing anti-anxiety and antioxidant properties are turmeric (curcumin as an active ingredient) and ginger.

Attaining Better Mental Health Through Diet

Always talk to your doctor if you experience severe anxiety symptoms that last more than two weeks. Even if your doctor recommends therapy or medication, you could still decide whether adjusting your diet can help. Although nutritional psychiatry is not suitable for treating other ailments, the relationship between food, mood, and anxiety is gathering more and more attention.

Physical Exercise

Physical exercise can also help with stress reduction. Maintaining a regular exercise routine has been linked with improved mood, enhanced self-esteem, and enhanced energy levels. Maintaining an routine exercise can ease most of the symptoms linked with anxiety and panic.

In short, the body's reaction to anxiety and panic attacks can be reduced with regular physical exercise. Exercise has been said to help lower the intensity and frequency of panic attacks. Exercise also helps to release pent-up mental and physical tension and reduces the feeling of fear.

Chapter 8:
Mindfulness and Positive Thinking

I f you have dipped into the sector of positive psychology, you must have discovered the most popular topic of today, which is mindfulness. It is a broad part of human psychology, which has evolved in the last few years.

What is mindfulness?

It is nothing but the act of maintaining all the moments of your very own feelings, thoughts, surrounding environment along with bodily sensations via the lens of nurturing and gentle nature. Every human being in this world is wired toward negativity. You can easily get caught up in the cycle of rumination, along with worrying and imagining about every possible outcome of your future. This often leads to an increased amount of anxiety along with lots of stress.

But, when you keep all your thoughts moving in the direction of positiveness, it will not only make you feel good at that very moment, but it can also help in reducing your degree of sadness to a great extent. Moreover, it can also provide the only thing that all human beings require for keeping up with their lives: HOPE. The more you engage yourself in employing positive thinking and mindfulness in your life, the longer the efforts will be lasting.

Meditation Based on Mindfulness

You must have come across the term "mindfulness meditation." If you think that the real difference between mindfulness and meditation is based on mindfulness, there isn't any such major difference. Mindfulness is meant to be generally incorporated into the life of an individual whereas meditation based on mindfulness is the most stereotypical form of meditation with you sitting with your legs crossed and eyes closed while engaging in the activity of basic meditation.

Typically, mindfulness meditation and mindfulness often refer to the same kind of concept in which you stay aware, open up your inner-self, and allow all your thoughts and feelings to occur without judgment. The only form of distinction which can be found between the two is that the concept of mindfulness meditation comes with the connotation of turning out to be a kind of practice that is time-constrained.

The most common question often found regarding mindfulness is whether it is a trait or a permanent state? This question is of utter importance for someone who dabbles in mindfulness.

Need for Mindfulness and Positive Thinking

Have you ever wondered about what it means to live in the present moment? All of us are indeed available right now at the current moment, but only 10% of us are right here. All of us are living within our minds and thoughts. Human beings exist in a state of day-to-daydreams where you are not connected with the world in actuality nor with your being. Instead, we are preoccupied with all our memories, busy churning our worries and thoughts about the future and the reactions and judgments of others. You miss out on most of your life, which ultimately leaves you feeling empty, shallow, and unsettled. That is when you need to learn to be mindful and to be at present. Let's look at some of the ways you can easily practice mindfulness in your regular life.

- Eating mindfully: When you gulp down your meal while being distracted by the computer, TV, or any form of constant conversation, you are missing out on the delicious taste and attractive smell of the food. You are also very less likely to feel nourished and satisfied after having a sumptuous meal as you missed out on the very fact of what you ate. In simple words, do not try to do 100 things at a time when sitting for your meal. Try to focus on what you are eating as it has been proven that when you eat well, you feel good. Having a tasty meal can make you feel positive and happy when you have a meal enjoyably.

- Walking down the road mindfully: There is a saying, "walk in a way as if you are embracing the earth right with your feet." In simple words, when you are out on the road alone, try to pay attention to all the significant movements of your body along with the surroundings. Notice the moment as your feet connect with the ground and then leave it again. All you need to do is observe what is going on around you. When you try to take a walk by yourself, you can connect with yourself in a better way than at any other point in time.

Try to feel everything around you: the sounds, sights, and lives that unfold. If you have negative thoughts or are just contemplating, try going out for a short walk where you can connect with your inner-self. You will be amazed to find out the results when you connect your heart with your mind like never before. You understand that you are your own best friend. So, try to connect with your inner friend to get the most out of your life and enjoy it to the fullest.

- Observing how you breathe: One single breath in and out can work like meditation. How you breathe occurs rhythmically and naturally. When you start to pay attention to how you breathe, it can take you right out of your mind and let you into your very own body. You will feel free momentarily from all the churning thoughts, fears, and worries in your mind, and you will recognize your true self by getting in touch with your inner soul and not with your regular thoughts.

- Connecting with all your senses: The human senses - smell, taste, touch, sight, and sound - are the gateway to the current moment. But when you remain lost in your thoughts, you will most likely not experience the things your senses are picking up for your mind. You can achieve this by doing the simplest things, such as pausing to soaking up the fantastic aroma of your coffee, the salty ocean wind, the diversity of your neighborhood, the beauty of flowers, and many others.

You can also achieve mindfulness by noticing how your clothing feels against your body, the clean and soft bed sheets on your skin every morning, the comfort you get as you kiss your lover, and various other wonderful things. All you need to do is just put a little amount of love and attention into the simplest tasks of your everyday life, and you will be amazed as you realize the amount of peace and joy you can bring up for yourself.

- Pause in between actions: You can pause during some of the simplest events in your life and listen to their inner meaning. You can pause and feel your body weight in the chair right before you start working at your desk. The primary goal is to give mini pauses to your life in between various actions throughout your day, which can help you reach out to your inner-self, clear up your mind, and provide you with a fresh form of energy for all the new tasks to come.

- Listening wholeheartedly: Most of us do not even listen to the people who speak to us just because we are engaged in what would be said next or just getting lost in the world of daydreams. The very next time you find yourself in a meaningful conversation, try to make it your primary goal to listen to what is being said by the other person instead of getting lost in your own thoughts. This will help you get the conversation's actual message, as mindfulness is all about living in the present.

- Getting lost in the flow of doing all the things you love: Every one of us has certain kinds of activities we love doing the most. Such activities help connect with our inner spirit and bring us alive. It can be dancing, cooking, gardening, singing, painting, writing, swimming, cycling, etc. People tend to love all those things they can lose themselves in. You can incorporate more flow in the activities of your daily routine to find your happiness reaching new heights.

- Meditating daily: Nothing can be better than meditation. When you start meditating regularly, you will come across various benefits like an increase in your happiness, energy, inner peace, and inspiration. When you find yourself getting lost in thoughts and you start overthinking, take some time to meditate. It is not needed to be more than 20 minutes, and even this amount of time can bring wonders. It can provide your life with a positive impact. It will help you strengthen your muscles of mindfulness so it becomes easier to be in the present moment throughout your day.

- Traveling or mixing up your entire routine: There are various reasons why people feel so amazing when on holidays. When you visit a new place, you become more mindful naturally and are in the present moment as there are new sounds, sights, and smells that you soak up. When you travel, your senses will take over your mind for a moment, resulting in freeing your mind right. Do you have any travel plans currently? No worries, as you can mix up your entire routine to have the same kind of effect.

Take a different road, stop by a new café, visit a newly opened place, or opt for something you haven't done before like cooking without anyone's help, scuba diving, and various other activities. When you opt for new activities at regular intervals, you will find yourself more confident and creative than before, and your mind will open to new opportunities.

- Observing all your emotions and thoughts: You are not your thoughts but the observer of all your thoughts. The very fact that you listen them depicts they are not you. You are someone separate and much higher. When you be aware of your thoughts and observe without judgmental eyes, you can be a part of the present. As you observe your thoughts, you are required to resists all your temptations and get carried away. Do not just get carried away with your thoughts.

Benefits of Practicing Mindfulness

Mindfulness comes with several benefits. Studies have found out that mindfulness can alter the human physiology of the mind and body so they can be healed, strengthened, and protected. Let's have a look at some of the benefits of practicing mindfulness.

- Lowers stress: Mindfulness helps lower your physiological markers of deep stress and helps improve the brain's ability to manage stress. It is done by improving the connectivity to those areas of your brain that are essential for executing control.

- Helps in restoring emotional balance: Emotional incidents can knock you down from your balance. The damage done comes in a great intensity, which can devastate your mental makeup. Mindfulness helps improve your recovery from any emotional situation simply by keeping a check on the emotional part of the brain.

- Helps reduce anxiety: It has been found from various studies that mindfulness can reduce the degree of anxiety in adults by up to 40%. It is done by increasing the amount of activity in that part of the brain that processes all the emotional and cognitive forms of information. That part of the brain controls the situations of worrying.

- Helps reduce physical pain: It has been proved that mindfulness can easily reduce physical pain without even activating the opioid system of the body. It also helps in reducing the potential for any side effects of an addictive nature. This is beneficial if you experience physical pain often and is particularly helpful for those who have built up a good tolerance for opiate-based drugs.

- Helps in reducing depression: It readily helps in dealing with depression. It helps open up your mind so you can soak in all the positive energy from your surroundings and feel more motivated.

- Helps improve sleep quality: You can easily improve your sleep quality by regularly practicing mindfulness. It also helps in reducing fatigue along with insomnia.

- It helps improve concentration: It helps improve attention and your ability to concentrate on your tasks. Mindfulness helps ignore all forms of distraction, those most likely to act as the barriers in your way to success. Mindfulness comes with the same effects as undergoing therapy from a therapist. It helps build a positive form of energy, which ultimately improve your senses.

Chapter 9:

Remove Negative Influences

E verybody needs to carry on a progressively positive life. However, constant negative impacts are attempting to stop you. They may originate from inside you or outside. Any place they originate impacts your inspiration, self-assurance, and joy. It could be a companion or relative who condemn you or a terrible propensity that you cannot shake.

I offer step-by-step instructions to cut down those negative influences from your life to be a more positive person. Negative ideas keep you down and you cannot resist the urge to expect the worse. Be that as it may, you do not need terrible impacts to govern your life. On the off chance that you need to prevent them from controlling you, you have to remove them. In any case, this is not a simple activity, so do not let it get you down if you cannot change. Pursue disposing of the negative impacts throughout your life and begin living more decidedly.

Changing Your Lifestyle

Other individuals aren't the main things that massively affect your life. You get into negative behavior patterns that impact your decisions. Look at your life and see what has begun managing how you live. If you admit to and attempt to deal with addictions, for example, you can become a more joyful and increasingly secure individual. It does not make a difference if you change your association with people or go on for a detox. Nothing will make you feel you need to do change, but you. Change those destructive impacts and great positive alternatives through various new interests, exercise, and social mingling. It is about tackling your way of life. When conditions are making you think adversely, it is much simpler to transform them than to change yourself. If your activity is making you miserable and you keep failing, begin searching for another one. Address the things that control your life and chip away at them now.

Encircle Yourself with Positive People

The general population can tremendously affect us so why not be selective. Get rid of anyone who brings you down and expel them from your life. A few people in your family or at work are unavoidable, of course, but cut off negative associations as you can. If not, manage and offset them with positive people.

In a relationship, such an intense move is hard to return from. Cutting a companion is tough but not encumbered by family or work issues. Make sure that you are making the correct move when removing somebody who is unfeeling, damaging, or careless.

Some antagonistic individuals are unavoidable like associates you cannot coexist with, your closest companion's irritating best friend, or a relative you need to see on special occasions. When you cannot expel somebody from your life or choose not to, you figure out how to manage them, or you could wind up with negative people who influence your life. One of them is to grin and bear it, disregarding their inherent evil. Be that as it may, you cannot utilize this strategy all the time. For example, when you have to remain connected with others at work, offer a positive attitude and remind yourself that issues are their concern.

When compelled to have antagonistic individuals in your life, encircle yourself with constructive individuals and avert others' antagonism with newfound positivity.

Cut Negative Influences and be a More Positive Person

You cannot dispose of al negative circumstances or people. However, you can concentrate on more beneficial things. Perhaps you had a horrendous day, yet somebody was benevolent enough to hold a door open for you at work. Maybe you haven't figured out how to lose weight for some time no matter how many diets you have tried. Positive thinking is tied to beneficial things in so many spheres. It can battle negative people and thinking by not giving them a chance to govern your life.

Battling Negative Thinking

You can change your way of life if you think in an increasingly positive manner and manage negative contemplations appropriately. Keeping away from antagonistic individuals assists with this, yet you additionally must glimpse further inside yourself. Probably the best activity to improve your life is to define your objectives so you have something to pursue. You have to remain on track and assess the origins of any negativity.

Chapter 10:

Tools for Your Mind

I t seems a bit impractical, right? When you are totally scared and overburdened by stress, one thing you will not want to do is to think about the worst possible scenario. Our minds tell us convincing stories. Our thoughts are powerful enough to decide what we do or do not do. One method of controlling overthinking is to imagine the worst possible scenario.

If you are overthinking, there will be an increase in your mental effort, which will negatively influence your performance. Making plans for a difficult situation ensures you are prepared for any bad feeling during the event, so you prepare yourself to maximize all your potential. To redirect your thoughts into more positive ones, here are three short personal affirmations. By using one or more, you can achieve calmness and continue.

"It is not happening presently." Sure, an unfortunate event might likely happen, but it is not happening presently. This statement might help you become aware that, presently, you are unharmed.

"No matter what happens, I can handle it." This phrase makes you aware of your internal resources and motivates you to overcome life's problems. This idea is from the tradition of Cognitive Behavioral Therapy.

"I am responsible for my problems. Can I put an end to it?" The first section of this phrase originated from the Four Noble Truths of

Buddhism. A few times, I say to myself, "I am responsible for my problems! Again!!" I use this phrase so often that I now have shortened it to "responsible for own problems." This helps me save time.

The second part of the phrase, "Can I put an end to it?", has its origin from motivational studies advising that you are more likely to be encouraged by asking yourself a question rather than saying, "I can put an end to this" or judgmental, "Avoid causing more problems for yourself" as this only creates additional problems. The simple question, "Can I put an end to this?" makes you aware that it is up to you to make the choice. If there is an unfortunate event likely to happen, perhaps a death in the family, a divorce, or a natural disaster, the ideal thing to do will be to ask yourself, "What is the best thing to get ready if this ever happens?" Making preparations for your action plan can be a relief from worry.

If you are responsible for your problems, ask yourself, "what if" questions, admit these thoughts, comfort yourself with one of those statements mentioned earlier, and then keep moving. If you discover that your thoughts are wandering to your favorite tragic thoughts, do not be discouraged. Making changes in your thinking habits might be difficult, and lapses are expected. In reality, controlling tragic thoughts is a project that can last a lifetime. Yet, positive self-affirmations can help you overcome the "what if's" very quickly so you can concentrate your thoughts on the things that are important.

What to do When Considering the Worst-Case Scenario

Since I am the true child of my mother, thinking of the worst possible scenario comes naturally. How can I prevent this since that kind of thinking is ingrained in my DNA? So be aware that your worst is only your worst. What you regard as your worst possible scenario is exclusively based on your personal experiences and knowledge. Strictly speaking, there is always someone facing a more terrible situation. So, your worst might not even be the worst possible scenario.

Know that you do not know the worst. Don't believe you know the worst. A long time ago, my mother told me that she created the worst possible scenario that could happen. And like I told my mother, it is difficult to come up with ALL the possibilities. Stop trying to; it is just impossible.

Re-channel your energy. It can be very draining to come up with all the worst possible scenarios. If you expend so much energy on thinking, no energy is left for actually taking action. So, channel your "What if?" energy into concentrating on taking steps. Come to terms with the worst. The worst can take place, and it can be awful. You are not learning if you are not hurt in some way. So, if the worst-case takes place, come to terms with it and learn from it.

Why You Should Consider the Worst-Case Scenario

Sometimes when we get to the root of our utmost fear, we become aware that it is not really scary. If you are forced to become innovative, your suffering can yield positive results, create a solution, and help overcome your challenges. There are some reasons why this is effective for a lot of people. It enables you to come back to the present moment. Most times, when we feel scared, it is because we allow our brain to run wild with all the possible scenarios. Thinking about the worst possibility and coming to terms with it helps bring you back to the present moment. It creates the space needed to assess your thoughts and weigh the possibilities. When we assess those things that are very important to us, we explain the fear by asking ourselves, "What are the possibilities that this thing I am scared of will happen?" You can also assess your thoughts thoroughly with some basic questions.

Eventually, it enables you to process your thoughts, even if the worst comes to pass, you know you will still be fine. For many "ifs," we want to know the next step to take that will not drive us to the darkest parts of the earth. When we assess the worst possibility, taking that next step will be easier. Eventually, attempts to guarantee our safety and physiological stress response provides an excellent tool. It is important to assess the stress to be sure that the worst possibility is actually the worst, and the best thing to do when facing problems is to come up with solutions. Learn to move according to the flow, surrender to the wind, and take charge.

Chapter 11:

Tools for Creative Thinking

You can turn to get your creative energies pumping. Here is how:

- Prepare, pose inquiries, and absorb new inputs. Your mind resembles a sponge. Keep the ground fruitful by being interested, posing inquiries, and testing and investigating.

- Feed your brain by perusing great books, tuning in to music, or going to the theater. You can open up your mind to imaginative thinking through the wonders of others. The mind will make associations and draw bits of knowledge from so many sources.

- Keep a notepad of thoughts and bits of knowledge: Inspiration can strike you at any time. Record arbitrary musings and experiences when they jump out at you. These will turn into the crude material upon which to construct further thoughts.

- Allow yourself to commit errors: Inventiveness inevitably causes mistakes. Unless you take chances, you never figure out how to think innovatively. Innovativeness requires an experimentation. You should be ready to face snags and disappointments.

- Get physical exercise: A vigorous run or a session of tennis or swimming is an extraordinary way to support innovativeness. The endorphins discharged through exercise create a vibe that promotes brain creativity. So, get yourself off that lounge chair and go for a run.

- Bask in the lap of nature: Nature is our best instructor. She rouses us to think in new ways. Go for a stroll and find yourself a peaceful spot to do some reflection amid the greenery. Your creative mind will be energized, and you will discover your imagination restored. Thoughts come all the more effectively when we are in a loose and relaxing condition.

- Take a short rest: Your subliminal mind creates images in the semi-waking state. Enjoy a brief session of shut-eye while in your work area. As you float between a state of rest and awakening, your subliminal mind is dynamic, and thoughts come up naturally.

- Search for inspiration: Walk around any environment, converse with people and see what inspires you. This will challenge your old presumptions and offer a new perspective.

- Write down bits of data and knowledge. Later you can sort out and arrange these to frame new ideas. Problems are actually concealed chances, and limitations help the imagination. Brainstorm and debate ideas to produce new thoughts.

- Assess these thoughts through new agendas. You have to break down and test your thoughts for their practicality. Get input from your steady collaborators, with the goal that you can stimulate your own thoughts with their usage.

Innovativeness Tools

#1. Biomimicry is an innovative device procedure where you duplicate nature's thoughts to solve human issues. Here nature is treated as an answer supplier. Inventiveness tips and strategies can apply to most anything, as nature's creatures have advanced over the years and are reliable sources of knowledge and inspiration.

#2. Six Thinking Hats is an inventiveness instrument you can utilize when you need various modes of thinking. It very well may be utilized for investigating thoughts to choose which one to take forward. Six nonexistent hats hued dark, white, green, red, yellow and blue, indicating a few qualities. There is a significance for each shading. Use them to break down thoughts by referencing the hat they are dissecting.

#3. Traditional Brainstorming is an innovative apparatus method. You record an issue on a flipchart or board so everybody involved comprehends the issue. As people offer ideas, the facilitator records their thoughts. There is no rebuff or assessment of these thoughts. The looks for an accord on what thoughts can be viewed further.

#4. Quality Listing is where you separate an issue into littler bits and see what you discover. The initial step is to rundown the qualities of a specific item, for instance, a toothbrush. Think about both positive and negative aspects of each property of the article, for instance, the edges, bristles, and the entire state of the toothbrush. Finally, look at altering the characteristics somehow changing the negative qualities. This innovativeness apparatus method is useful in the planning of new models.

#5. The Osborn Checklist yields new arrangements from existing thoughts. You need to apply the accompanying inquiries to the arrangement:

- Substitute?
- Adopt?
- Magnify/minimize?
- Combine?
- Rearrange?
- Modify?
- Any other use?

#6. Wishing is a strategy for creating radical thoughts and of thinking fresh ones. You extend your thinking past the sensible and the possible. You should be at your imaginative best. The initial step is to offer thoughts like, "I Wish," and after that thoughts of, "Wouldn't it be decent if."

#7. Negative Selection is an innovative apparatus method of arranging thoughts. You survey the issue to perceive what you are attempting to accomplish. At that point, you sort thoughts into "No" and "Possibly" classifications. You think about all parts of actualizing the thought such the cost, usage and purpose, and so forth. The object is to list the best thoughts with the most prominent odds of worthiness.

#8. Improvement Checklist is a schedule intended to break down a thought and prepare it for usage. The means molding, fitting, adjusting, fortifying, dissecting potential deformities, contrasting current circumstances, and preparing the industrial model.

#9. Individual Analogy is inventiveness device system that represents speed or lifelessness as related to ideas or articles. You take an idea and embody it, giving it human feelings and sentiments. At that point, you impart the representation and feelings and connections through pretending or pictures. The following stage is to make associations between the simple and the subject. Record bits of knowledge picked up.

#10. Supposition Challenging involves innovativeness tips and strategy to take new points of view at things. It pursues a three-advance procedure:

- Take a basic segment of your concern.
- Record the suspicions around it.
- Challenge these by saying, "What if that was not there..."
- Answer the inquiry from a new viewpoint.

Chapter 12:

Suggestions for Living More Mindfully

I t might be easy to devote several book to how you can better support your meditation practice, but I mention here what I find to be a few of the most important in the hope that they will help to improve your mindfulness in your day-to-day life. Of course, the theme is one of perception, or an appreciation of one and the other. We need to cultivate a gentle curiosity to look at, consider, and observe what happens in every part of your life— how you behave, how you talk, and how you think. Yet note, it's not about pretending to be someone; it's about having a sense of peace with you right now as you are.

1. Perspective- choosing how you see your life

It doesn't matter how you see your life for meditation to be successful. But it can be helpful to understand the general trend, so you can be more sensitive to the urge to fall into negative thought patterns. And this greater understanding provides the opportunity for positive change.

It's also helpful to note how your attitude can shift: how one day you can go on a busy train and not be overly concerned about every button you have to press. What's positive here is that it's not what happens outside us that is most troublesome, but what happens in our thoughts— which, luckily, can change. Noticing these changeable viewpoints from day to day and moment to moment will strongly help your daily meditation.

2. Contact with other people

It is impossible to encourage calm and open minds to take out your grievances on others if you want to achieve a greater sense of satisfaction by meditation. So, it is crucial to interact skillfully and sensitively with others et some headspace. It may mean that your relationships become more balanced, empathic, or perspective— or maybe all three!

3. Appreciation—smelling the roses

That said, some people still want to fight no matter how well-intended they are. In these cases, you can always choose to do nothing. Trying to feel relaxed and considering similar mental problems in yourself can be very beneficial. Still, if anyone is rude regularly, it would be better to stay away if you could. Have you ever noticed how much focus some people place on even the least little challenge in their lives and how little time they spend talking about moments of happiness? Some explanation for this is that satisfaction is "all ours" somehow and everything else is wrong or out of place.

Some people feel guilty for taking time off, but it is necessary if we want to have more headspace. When there is a clear sense of pride in life, it is incredibly difficult to get lost in distracting thoughts. We also start to see more clearly what is lacking in the lives of others by having a deeper understanding of what we have.

4. Kindness — into yourself as well as to others

It feels nice to be kind to anyone else. It's not rocket science. It looks useful and right to you. It makes for a calm and healthy mind. But while you are there, how about demonstrating to yourself some kindness — especially as you learn to be more conscious. Today, we live in a world with such high standards that we can objectively discover something new about our success.

Fortunately, meditation has a weird way of bringing out people's kindness, and the daily practice of goodness feeds into your meditation. It makes the mind deeper and more comfortable. It produces an attitude that is less judgmental and more reasonable. It has significant implications for our relationships with others.

5. Compassion—in the shoes of others

Compassion is not something we can "do" or "make" in other people's shoes; it already exists in each one of us. The same idea applies to kindness if you think back to the blue-sky example. In reality, you might say that the blue sky is in equal measure consciousness and compassion.

Compassion happens naturally when the clouds expose the blue sky. We have to make a conscientious effort that looks a little more like the blue sky, even though the clouds overshadow it during other moments. The more you picture this situation, the more realistic it becomes. Compassion is just like empathy - putting oneself in another's shoes and possessing a shared sense of understanding.

6. Balance— a sense of equanimity

Life is not unlike the sea, ebbing and flowing all our lives. Yes, it is often peaceful and serene, but the waves can be so massive at other times that they threaten to overwhelm us. Such variations represent an inevitable part of life. But when you forget this fundamental reality, massive waves of challenging emotions are quickly swept away.

It is possible to cultivate a positive attitude by practicing mind meditation to feel a greater sense of serenity in life. It should not be mistaken for a bland existence where you float like an emotionless gray blob through your life. Currently, it's quite the opposite. Through a better understanding of your feelings, your perception will be improved. You won't feel like you're at the mercy of anything because you're less trapped.

7. Acceptance—resistance is futile

No matter how lucky the conditions, life can be frustrating and demanding at times. We tend to ignore this and feel discouraged and depressed because we don't have a way of doing things ourselves. Like compassion, it can be helpful to focus on acceptance in the blue sky analogy.

In this sense, the path to acceptance is to figure out what we have to let go of, and not what we have to continue to do. You will begin to understand what prevents recognition from occurring spontaneously by observing moments of resistance during the day. In effect, it will help you see more quickly the thoughts and feelings that emerge during your meditation.

8. Composure—letting go

Life has become so busy and so hectic, that an anxious feeling might be unavoidable. During these times, you might feel your jaw tightening, a foot tightening, or a slow breath. Yet, the very essence of it starts to shift by understanding impatience accompanied with a strong sense of curiosity. The momentum slows down somehow, and its grasp is released.

Impatience is as likely to surface in daily life as in your meditation practice—one represents the other. If you are like most people, you may well ask, "Why don't I experience results faster? "But note that meditation isn't about success and performance, which is why it differs from the rest of life. It is more about learning to be awake, to rest with a real sense of ease in this domain of natural consciousness.

9. Dedication—sticking with it

Mindfulness is a profound change in the way you communicate with your thoughts and feelings. Although it can sound exciting or daunting, it is done by repeating the exercise. It means daily meditation, no matter how you feel. Unlike any other skill, the more often you submit to it, the more relaxed and comfortable you become with a renewed sense of consciousness.

By practicing in this way — little and often — you will slowly create a healthy consciousness in your meditation that naturally flows into the rest of your life. Similarly, it can have a positive impact on your practice by becoming more conscious of daily life. When you are specifically inspired and mindful of why you practice meditation and who those around you are likely to benefit from your better sense of headspace, it is unlikely that you will have trouble sitting down for 10 minutes a day.

10. Presence—living life skillfully

Living skillfully means that you can control yourself when you think you will say or do something you might regret later. It also means having the power and maturity of perception rather than responding impulsively to challenging situations. A skillful living, therefore, requires a certain amount of racial wisdom.

Conclusion

S o what are you waiting for? I know it's hard to get out of the "overthinking" habit, but once you train yourself to think about things more simply and logically, you won't have it anymore!

"Remembering that there's a world outside your head is the main step to relief." – Albert Camus.

All overthinking does is make your life more complicated. And keep in mind that most of your worries can be solved with a little bit of action. You don't need to overthink everything if you take charge and do something about it! No matter how minor or major the problem may seem, taking action will always help somehow. So, get out of your head and take action.

"Don't let the perfect be the enemy of the good." – Voltaire

Now that you know this, don't just sit there and try to find your problems in life. Overthinking about them doesn't help at all. Just take some action as soon as you can, and let things work themselves out.

"The next best thing to solving a problem is finding some humor in it." – Ethel Barrymore.

When you, at last, permit yourself to let go of your worries, you'll be able to move along with your life with much more ease. And remember, too much stress isn't good for anyone. When you learn how to stop overthinking, you'll find peace in your life as well.

"To think is easy. To act is hard. But the hardest thing in the world is to act following your thinking. " – Johann Wolfgang von Goethe.

And, remember one more thing. When you stop overthinking about everything, you'll be able to enjoy the simple things in life a lot more. Enjoying the simple things in life is one of the most important parts of a happy life, and when you learn how to stop overthinking, it will become easier and easier each day.

"Count your age by friends, not years. Count your life by smiles, not tears." – Anonymous

www.ingramcontent.com/pod-product-compliance
Lightning Source LLC
Chambersburg PA
CBHW071113030426
42336CB00013BA/2066